D0526585

The Old Testament
and the Archaeologist

FRONTISPIECE A.   THE SOLOMONIC GATE AT GEZER

FRONTISPIECE B.   THE JOINT IN THE EAST WALL OF THE
HARAM ESH-SHARIF

The Old Testament and the Archaeologist

by
H. Darrell Lance

First published 1981 by Fortress Press, USA
First published in Great Britain 1983
SPCK
Holy Trinity Church
Marylebone Road
London NW1 4DU

Copyright © Fortress Press 1981

Biblical quotations in this publication are from the Revised Standard Version of the Bible, copyright 1946, 1952, © 1971, 1973 by the Division of Christian Education of the National Council of the Churches of Christ in the USA, and are used by permission.

ISBN 0 281 04021 4

Printed in Great Britain by Ebenezer Baylis and Son Ltd
The Trinity Press, Worcester, and London

Contents

Abbreviations

AASOR	Annual of the American Schools of Oriental Research
AJA	*American Journal of Archaeology*
BA	*Biblical Archeologist*
BARev	*Biblical Archaeology Review*
BASOR	*Bulletin of the American Schools of Oriental Research*
EAEHL	Avi-Yonah, Michael, and Stern, Ephraim, eds. *Encyclopedia of Archaeological Excavations in the Holy Land.* 4 vols. Englewood Cliffs, N.J.: Prentice Hall; and Jerusalem: Israel Exploration Society and Massada Press, 1975–78.
EI	*Eretz-Israel*
IEJ	*Israel Exploration Journal*
JAOS	*Journal of the American Oriental Society*
JBL	*Journal of Biblical Literature*
JNES	*Journal of Near Eastern Studies*
OIC	Oriental Institute Communications
OIP	Oriental Institute Publications
PEQ	*Palestine Exploration Quarterly*
ZAW	*Zeitschrift für die alttestamentliche Wissenschaft*

Illustrations

ACKNOWLEDGMENTS

Permission to reproduce the following illustrations is gratefully acknowledged: Frontispiece B—the Jerusalem Excavations; Fig. 6— J. D. Seger; Figs. 8 and 10—Yigael Yadin; Fig. 9—Palestine Exploration Fund. Fig. 7 is after Robert S. Lamon and Geoffrey M. Shipton, *Megiddo I: Seasons of 1925–34*, OIP 42 (Chicago: University of Chicago Press, 1939), Fig. 3. Fig. 12 is after Kathleen M. Kenyon, *Digging Up Jerusalem* (London & Tonbridge: Ernest Benn, 1974), Fig. 22.

Glossary

Ashlar—Building stone which has been shaped into squared blocks; masonry built of such stones.

Assemblage—The sum total of different types, such as pottery, weapons, house plans, and so on, which are characteristically found together, for example, in a stratum.

Balk—An unexcavated strip, usually 1 meter in width, left standing between areas in order to preserve temporarily a sample of the stratification. The face of the balk provides a section, q.v.

Burnish—A technique of polishing pottery by applying pressure with a tool, such as a bone, shell, or other instrument, to the leather-hard clay before firing. It can be continuous over the whole vessel or in various patterns. Irregular marks indicate hand burnishing; wheel burnishing produces regular rings.

Carbon dating—The dating of organic matter through measurement of the surviving proportion of the radioisotope carbon-14. The uncertainties inherent in this method make it more useful for prehistoric than for historic periods.

Epigraphy—The study of ancient written remains, their classification, dating, and interpretation.

Fill—Tell debris or virgin soil brought in by the ancient inhabitants of a site to fill pits and holes, to level uneven ground, and so on.

Graffito (s.), Graffiti (pl.)—Drawings or writing scratched on a surface of stone, plaster, pottery, or other object.

Horizon—A term usually used in Palestinian archaeology to designate a broad chronological period or cultural phase.

In situ—Undisturbed; in its original "site" or place.

Leveling rod—A rod marked in regular units used with a surveyor's instrument to measure heights.

Locus (s.), Loci (pl.)—A term used by different archaeologists to mean different things. Very often it refers to a room or other large architectural feature. It is used in this volume to refer to the smallest coherent unit of stratigraphy—layer, wall, floor, and so on—which can be distinguished from all others. See Chapter II.

Midden—A garbage and refuse heap.

Mound—Usually means the same as tell, q.v.

Offsets–insets—A type of city wall which is constructed in sections, with each section set slightly back or forward in relation to the one adjacent. The technique is designed to limit damage to the wall to one or two sections rather than letting it spread to a long stretch.

Ostracon (s.), Ostraca (pl.)—A potsherd used as writing material. Can be incised or written in ink. Contents are nearly always ephemera—letters, lists, receipts, and so on.

Palaeography—The study of the typology of ancient scripts; one aspect of epigraphy.

Phase—Often used in archaeology with its broad meaning of a stage or interval in an ongoing development; more specifically, a stage within the life of a stratum. A stratum may reveal several phases, some of which may have subphases.

Robber, robbing—The removal of building stone from out-of-use structures; especially used to refer to pits dug into earlier strata to search for stone.

Section—A cut through something, often made to reveal its internal structure; a scale drawing of something revealed in section, often the stratification of the mound revealed in the face of a balk, q.v.

Slip—A thin layer of fine clay applied as a veneer to a pot before it is fired.

Stele—A standing stone with carved decoration, inscription, or both.

Stratigraphy—The analysis of stratified materials; specifically the analysis of the sequence of layers, buildings, and other features as they came into existence in the formation of a mound.

Stratum—A major stage in the life of a stratified site; a coherent level of occupation, usually separated from earlier and later strata by layers of fill or destruction. See section on "The Formation of the Mound" in Chapter II.

Tell, also Tel—An ancient site, built up of successive layers or strata of occupation, often in the form of a small hill with a flat top.

Terminus ad quem—The latest limits; the limits before which something must be dated. The terminus ad quem for a royal seal of Israel would be 722–21 B.C. when the kingdom of Israel ceased to exist.

Terminus ante quem—Same as terminus ad quem, q.v.

Terminus a quo—The earliest limits; the limits after which something must be dated. The terminus a quo for a royal seal of Israel would be the rebellion of Jeroboam early in the reign of Solomon's son, Rehoboam, since Israel did not exist as a separate kingdom before then.

Terminus post quem—Same as *terminus a quo,* q.v.

Theodolite—A surveyor's instrument equipped with a telescope which can be adjusted to exact horizontal and vertical attitudes; used in archaeology to make contour maps, to lay out areas of excavation, and to calculate vertical heights of excavated features in relation to a fixed point.

Tip line—Sloping lines formed by debris dumped down an incline; most clearly seen in section (see Fig. 2).

Type—Simply defined, a group of objects or other cultural features which can be classified together because they share certain important characteristics.

Typology—The study and classification of types, q.v.

I

Archaeology
and the Old Testament

The recovery of century upon century of lost human history through archaeological exploration, excavation, and decipherment over the last two hundred years is one of the astonishing achievements of the modern age. Apart from tales of occasional travelers, medieval Europe was as unaware of the existence of the splendors of ancient Egypt as it was of the Rocky Mountains. All ideas about human history before the Greeks were based on the Bible plus some indirect and secondhand information in a few classical writers such as Herodotus, Josephus, and Eusebius.

It was out of Europe's expansion and quest for empire that it finally learned that there still existed impressive and abundant remains of civilizations far older than Greece and Rome. When Napoleon invaded Egypt in 1798 he took with him scholars and draftsmen whom he directed to make a survey of ancient monuments. They succeeded nobly, publishing their results in the sumptuous volumes of *La Description de l'Égypte* which for the first time revealed to the eyes of Europe's astonished intelligentsia the existence of monuments and art rivaling those of Europe itself.

But of far greater importance in the long run was an accidental find by some of Napoleon's soldiers at a place called Rosetta on the Nile Delta. It was a trilingual inscription of King Ptolemy V Epiphanes written in Greek and in both forms of the Egyptian language, hieroglyphic and demotic. For the first time it was indisputable that the curious pictorial markings which covered Egyptian monuments were in fact a form of writing, and some of Europe's best brains set to work to decipher it through the key of the Greek version of the Rosetta stone. It was the young French scholar Jean François Champollion who finally broke the system. By steeping himself in Coptic, the surviving descendant of the language of ancient Egypt, and building on the sugges-

1

tions of others, he succeeded brilliantly in deciphering the writing system and in laying the foundation for a full recovery of the ancient language. The virtually endless inscriptions that covered the walls of the tombs and temples of ancient Egypt were gradually forced to speak.

Skipping over Palestine for the moment, we move around the semi-circle of habitable lands on the fringe of the Syrian desert—the lands which have been called the Fertile Crescent—until we come to Mesopotamia, today mostly occupied by the nation of Iraq. Unlike Egypt, few prominent monuments survived in this flat barren plain between the Tigris and Euphrates rivers to indicate past glory. However, random finds plus intriguing reports by early travelers and explorers stimulated interest in the many mounds which dotted the landscape. In 1842 Paul-Émile Botta, the vice-consul for France at Mosul in northern Mesopotamia, began excavations at what proved to be the site of Khorsabad, the capital of the Assyrian king Sargon II. An Englishman, A. H. Layard, followed suit at Calah, Nineveh, and Assur; and the flow of massive sculptures and reliefs from the Assyrian period to the museums of the West began in earnest. Although these early explorations were often little better than treasure hunts and highly destructive in their methods, they aroused interest among scholars all across Europe. The writing system used in Mesopotamia, syllabic signs made up of wedge-shaped (cuneiform) marks in various combinations, proved more difficult to crack than had Egyptian hieroglyphs; but it gradually yielded, revealing that cuneiform was not a single language but a system of writing which had been used for a number of different, sometimes quite unrelated languages, such as Sumerian (related to no other known language), Akkadian (a language of the Semitic family), and Hittite (an Indo-European language). An enormous quantity of cuneiform material has survived because the normal medium of writing, apart from royal or monumental inscriptions, was clay, shaped usually into flat rectangular tablets. Once sun-dried, clay tablets become very durable and, if baked, nearly indestructible. Consequently, not only have governmental and religious documents survived but also the letters and business records of ordinary citizens, thus permitting a reconstruction of everyday life in Mesopotamia that is more detailed in most respects than our knowledge of ancient Greece or Rome.

In contrast to those of Egypt and Mesopotamia, the material culture of Palestine during most ancient periods was poor, leaving no impressive monuments or artistic treasures to attract modern attention. As the Holy Land, Palestine had always drawn pilgrims and crusaders, but their interest in the ancient places was largely pious. The first person to come to Palestine with modern eyes, systematically asking modern questions, was an American, Edward Robinson. He made two trips of exploration to Palestine in 1838 and 1852, identifying hundreds of ancient sites and laying the groundwork for further exploration. Random investigation and discovery continued throughout the nineteenth century—the Moabite stone in 1868, the Siloam inscription in 1880—but the first systematic excavation of an ancient mound did not take place until 1890 when an Egyptologist, Sir Flinders Petrie, dug part of a site in the southern coastal plain called Tell el-Ḥesī.

From these beginnings—and similar stories could be told about Syria, Anatolia, and Phoenicia with its settlements throughout the Mediterranean—there has flowed a widening and deepening stream of information about the ancient past, the world we now usually call the "ancient Near East," the world in which the Israelite nation lived and the Old Testament originated. No longer is the Bible the sole witness to the earliest human history; for as Friederich Delitzsch dramatically expressed in his controversial "Babel-Bible" lecture of 1902, "the pyramids have opened their depths and the Assyrian palaces their portals" and the Bible now takes its place in a vast and increasingly complex pattern.[1]

Above all, therefore, what archaeology—using that term loosely for the moment to refer to the sum total of all our new information about the cultures of the ancient Near East—has done for the interpretation of the Old Testament is to give it a contemporary setting and context. Without such a setting, even assuming the rise of critical scholarship, our understanding of the Old Testament would have been distorted forever, like peering down a long tunnel through a monocular telescope, a tiny and confusing view without perspective or context. What archaeology has done is to give us that necessary context—historical, cultural, linguistic, and religious.

To illustrate the pivotal importance of this achievement, we need only contrast the interpretation of Genesis 1 by two giants in the history of biblical interpretation whose careers overlapped each other as well as the period when the significance of the new discoveries was beginning to be discerned.

The name of Julius Wellhausen will forever be linked to the so-called documentary hypothesis which he defended so brilliantly, namely that the finished Pentateuch was a literary combination of four separate written sources, designated J, E, D, and P, and that it reached its pres-

1. *Babel and Bible*, trans. Thomas J. McCormack and W. H. Carruth (Chicago: Open Court Publishing Co., 1903), p. 3.

3

ent form only at the end of the Old Testament period, not at the beginning as the work of Moses. Wellhausen attributed Genesis 1, or more exactly Gen. 1:1—2:4a, to the latest of the sources, the Priestly writer (P), even as most scholars do to this day. However, according to Wellhausen's understanding of the four Pentateuchal sources, each source reflected the historical period in which it was actually written, which would mean that Genesis 1 must represent the theological outlook of Israel at its latest and most sophisticated period. As proof for the late date of Genesis 1, Wellhausen pointed, for example, to the sense of order in the stately progression of the seven days of creation. From the chaos of verse one, the rest of creation proceeds like a set of logical conclusions from a premise. The Priestly writer has systematically constructed the whole story out of his own reflection, building an ordered and logical universe.[2] In short, Wellhausen saw Gen. 1:1—2:4a as a conscious theological and cosmogonic statement, fabricated *de novo* out of whole cloth in the speculative abstract manner he believed to be typical of the Priestly writer.

Wellhausen's synthesis was brilliant, but it was constructed almost totally in isolation from any ancient comparative materials. The recovery of the contemporary Near Eastern context of the Bible had barely begun; and such information as was available, Wellhausen consciously ignored, believing that Israel's development was essentially independent of the development of Egypt or Babylonia.[3]

Only seventeen years after Wellhausen's *Prolegomena*, there appeared another treatment of Genesis 1 by Hermann Gunkel, a younger contemporary. Gunkel accepted the chapter as part of the P source but argued strongly against Wellhausen's theory of the origin of its ideas. In fact, one section of his comments is entitled "Gen. 1 is Not a Free Construction of the Author." In it Gunkel explicitly refutes Wellhausen by demonstrating element after element in the story for which there were parallels in the newly recovered folklore of other nations, especially in the Babylonian creation myth.[4] Reading these two nearly contemporary treatments of Genesis 1, one sees in retrospect that their views of the new archaeological material place them on opposite sides of a major watershed. Old Testament research would follow many paths in the future, but at least one thing was clear: no longer could the Old Testament be reliably interpreted as a self-contained system

2. Julius Wellhausen, *Prolegomena to the History of Ancient Israel*, trans. J. S. Black and A. Menzies (1885; reprint ed., New York: Meridian Books, 1957), p. 298.
3. William F. Albright, "Introduction" to Hermann Gunkel, *The Legends of Genesis* (New York: Schocken Books, 1964), pp. vii–viii.
4. Hermann Gunkel, *Schöpfung und Chaos in Urzeit und Endzeit* (Göttingen: Vandenhoeck und Ruprecht, 1895), pp. 4–16.

in isolation from the rest of the ancient Near East. Those who would understand the Bible in depth would have to read it as an organic part of its context.

Broadly speaking, there are two categories of archaeological evidence which together provide the raw material for our reconstruction of the ancient Near Eastern context: (a) written texts, ranging from complete epics to broken fragments of a word or two, and (b) artifactual material.

Mesopotamia and Egypt have been the major sources of written material, especially Mesopotamia. We have already mentioned that the common medium of writing in Mesopotamia was clay which when dried or baked survives with admirable tenacity. Scores of thousands of these tablets have been recovered. The earliest of these, the oldest written documents known, date from the last third of the fourth millennium B.C. Although all of this material is indispensable for the reconstruction of the history of that region, certain texts or groups of texts stand out as particularly important for biblical studies. A few examples will have to suffice.

One of the earliest groups of tablets discovered was from the seventh-century B.C. library in Nineveh of the Assyrian king Ashurbanipal. Something of an antiquary and proud of his ability to read, the king had instructed his scribes to seek out and make copies of earlier texts. Although chance turned up this library in the earliest years of the exploration of Mesopotamia, decipherment of the language was still in its infancy, and the tablets languished in the storerooms of the British Museum. It was not until 1872 that a museum worker, George Smith, made an electrifying discovery. Scanning one of the tablets, his startled eyes beheld a reference to a ship touching ground on a mountain called Nisir, and then these lines:

> When the seventh day arrived,
> I sent forth and set free a dove.
> The dove went forth, but came back;
> Since no resting-place for it was visible, she turned round.[5]

This was the first hint that the stories of Genesis might have parallels in other sources. The announcement of the discovery created a sensation. A London newspaper even sent Smith on an expedition to Nineveh to look for more fragments of the epic in which this version of the flood story occurred. Incredibly, within a few days after he

5. Trans. E. A. Speiser, *Ancient Near Eastern Texts*, ed. James B. Pritchard, 2d ed. (Princeton, N.J.: Princeton University Press, 1955), p. 94.

started new excavations, Smith in fact found a tablet which filled in the only serious break in the flood narrative. It was also Smith who in 1875 announced the finding of the Babylonian story of creation, *Enuma elish,* which had striking similarities to the first chapter of Genesis. We cannot take space to follow the story of discovery further; but to demonstrate that the end is nowhere in sight, we mention only the publication for the first time in 1969 of a relatively complete edition of the story of Atra-hasis in which the creation of humankind and its subsequent near-destruction by the gods in a flood occur together in the same narrative, a pattern much closer to the biblical narrative than anything previously known.[6]

Also from Mesopotamia have come collections of laws, the most famous being the eighteenth-century B.C. code of Hammurabi of Babylon, which have given us new perspectives on the legal sections of the Old Testament. From the archives of Mari on the upper Euphrates River has come information about tribal society among early Northwest Semitic peoples as well as on the backgrounds of the prophetic movement in later Israel. Monumental inscriptions of Assyrian kings have given us visual scenes of the sieges of biblical sites such as Gezer and Lachish. Sennacherib's annals recount from the Assyrian viewpoint the subjugation of King Hezekiah (cf. 2 Kings 18:13–15). And these examples do not begin to exhaust the range and depth of relevant materials.

In Egypt, the normal medium for writing was not clay but stone, wood, and papyrus (whence our word "paper"), made from the matted pith of the papyrus reed. The written material that has survived in Egypt is massive, as is that of Mesopotamia, though there is much less direct connection to the Old Testament. Many of the temple and tomb inscriptions give little information, being highly formulaic, endlessly repeating praise of the pharaoh or prayers for the afterlife. Nevertheless, the historical information from Egyptian sources is invaluable. The cuneiform Amarna tablets, found in the ruins of the short-lived capital of Pharaoh Amenophis IV, better known as Ikhnaton, give us intimate, albeit confused, information about the world of international relations in the early fourteenth century B.C. and specifically about the city-states of Canaan, then under nominal Egyptian control. Other sources, such as the Tale of Sinuhe of the twentieth century B.C., the Execration Texts of the same period and a little later, Papyrus Anastasi I of the mid-second millennium, and the story of Wen-Amon of about

---

6. W. G. Lambert and A. R. Millard, *Atra-hasis: The Babylonian Story of the Flood* (Oxford: Clarendon Press, 1969).

1100 B.C., provide glimpses of the geopolitics and everyday life of the region that was later to be called Palestine. And of course there are the monumental inscriptions, accounts of pharaonic exploits, such as the campaigns into Canaan of Thutmose III in the fifteenth century B.C. and Shishak in the tenth (see 1 Kings 14:25–28).

As for Syria, two groups of texts stand out above all others, those of Ugarit and Ebla. The study of the Ebla tablets, the total number of which is still unclear, has barely begun but will certainly cause the history of western Asia in the third millennium B.C. to be rewritten.[7] Also Ebla promises information about the mediation of Mesopotamian culture to Canaan in the period before the patriarchs and about earlier stages of the linguistic family of which Hebrew is a late development. But all this is yet to unfold. The Ugaritic materials, on the other hand, since their decipherment in 1930 have revolutionized our understanding of Canaanite religion and have clarified many obscure passages in the Bible. For example, the first line of Job 18:15 is unintelligible as it stands in the received Hebrew text. The Revised Standard Version reads

> In his tent dwells that which is none of his;
> brimstone is scattered upon his habitation.

Not only does the first line make no intrinsic sense, it forms no parallel to the second line after the customary style of Hebrew poetry. However, Mitchell Dahood has argued that the Hebrew phrase translated in the RSV as "that which is none of his" has been misunderstood and should be connected to a root *nbl* which occurs in Ugaritic and other Semitic languages with the meaning "to burn." Dahood thus translates

> Fire is set in his tent,
> Indeed sulphur is strewn on his dwelling,

a translation which commends itself not only by its sense and its restoration of the parallelism of the poetry but also because it requires no emendation of the Hebrew text. In short, we have an improved reading, thanks to the discoveries from Ugarit.[8]

Compared with the rest of the ancient Near East—and there are whole regions omitted from our examples—Palestine has produced little epigraphic material. Nevertheless, for biblical studies, the finds

---

7. It turns out that the early reports of 17,000 or more tablets referred to inventory numbers, not whole tablets; see most recently Robert Biggs, "The Ebla Tablets: An Interim Perspective," *BA* 43 (1980):80.
8. Mitchell Dahood, "Some Northwest–Semitic Words in Job," *Biblica* 38 (1957): 312–14.

have been of surpassing importance. No archaeological find since the opening of the tomb of Pharaoh Tutankhamen has so captured the popular imagination as the discovery of the Dead Sea Scrolls, found in caves near Khirbet Qumran on the northwestern shore of the Dead Sea. Actually the Qumran manuscripts are only one group, although certainly the major one, of leather and papyrus documents preserved by the arid climate of the Jordan Valley and recovered from caves and ruins located from Wadi Daliyeh north of Jericho to Masada toward the southern end of the Dead Sea, and dating from the fourth century B.C. to the eighth century A.D.[9] Although the scrolls and other materials have not produced the sensational results predicted for them by early and overenthusiastic press reports, the actual harvest of new information and insight, especially regarding Judaism around the turn of the common era, has been rich.

One can hope for manuscript finds only in the dry Jordan Valley. Elsewhere in Palestine the only written materials to survive the wet winters have been inscribed on stone, more rarely on metal, or else printed in ink on pieces of broken pottery (ostraca). From time to time the odd bit of cuneiform tablet turns up. But all these are rare. Except for a brief period under David and Solomon, Palestine has never been the seat of an important international power with the wealth to produce numerous monuments and inscriptions. Thus, apart from the occasional Egyptian stele, the best preserved monumental inscription is that of King Mesha of the Trans-Jordanian country of Moab (2 Kings 3:4). The Siloam inscription, beautifully carved in the flowing script typical of the eighth century B.C., is the closest thing we have to a royal Judean or Israelite inscription, describing the final stages of the digging of the Siloam tunnel under Jerusalem, probably by Hezekiah, to bring the waters of the spring Gihon within the safety of the city walls (2 Kings 20:20; 2 Chron. 32:30; Ecclus. 48:17). Apart from the Siloam inscription, the only other possible candidates for royal inscriptions are a few letters on a piece found in Jerusalem and a sad fragment from Samaria that contains but one word, 'ašer, the Hebrew relative pronoun "which" or "that."

The more common form of writing which has been preserved randomly and in several important caches, in Arad, Lachish, and Samaria,

---

9. For recent summaries with bibliographies see J. A. Sanders, "The Dead Sea Scrolls — A Quarter Century of Study", *BA* 36 (1973): 109–48; G. Vermes, "Dead Sea Scrolls", *The Interpreter's Dictionary of the Bible: Supplementary Volume* (Nashville: Abingdon Press, 1976), pp. 210–19; G. Vermes, *The Dead Sea Scrolls: Qumran in Perspective* (London: Collins, 1977).

is the ostracon, a smooth piece of broken pottery on which was written a message with pen and ink. Most of these are administrative records of one sort or another; but those from Lachish and Arad give us interesting and sometimes dramatic glimpses into the historical events of the time. Apart from the content of the inscriptions, these bits and pieces are of priceless value for studies in Hebrew grammar and orthography, giving us samples of Hebrew unaffected by the succeeding centuries of linguistic and textual change. As a reminder that discovery is a continual process, one might mention, for example, the major new find from Kuntilet 'Ajrud, a desert station on the road from Gaza to Eilat and Sinai. Preliminary reports indicate that not only are the finds considerable in quantity, they are mostly religious in content; and since they date from the time of the Judean monarchy, they will give us an unprecedented glimpse of the religious situation contemporary with the age of the great prophets.[10]

Written remains must, of course, be set in a category apart because of their ability to communicate directly. But written materials usually comprise the smallest percentage of the archaeologist's finds; sometimes an excavation—especially in Palestine—will produce little more than half a line of faint lettering on a broken sherd, perhaps a broken seal or two, and nothing more. Everything else that is found—walls, floors, cooking ovens, tools, weapons, industrial installations, jewelry, carbonized seeds, bones, and the ubiquitous pottery—is mute, presenting problems of interpretation quite different from written materials. But when properly excavated and interpreted (important conditions which we shall discuss in the next chapter), it is this category of find which allows us to reconstruct the life and culture of the people. The elegance or simplicity of the buildings can tell us something of economic conditions. Numerous wine vats reveal that a site was a center of viticulture. The seeds and bones tell us about the diet of the ancient inhabitants and the domestic animals they kept. Decorations on objects and pottery hint at their aesthetic sense. The presence of foreign objects indicates trade or foreign travel. Frequent destruction–layers reveal possibly unsettled political conditions. The picture reconstructed in this way, of course, is incomplete and skewed since all the perishable items of wood, cloth, and fiber have usually disappeared, except in very dry areas such as Egypt, Sinai, or near the Dead Sea. Nevertheless,

10. Ze'ev Meshel, "Did Yahweh Have a Consort? The New Religious Inscriptions from the Sinai," *BARev* 5, no. 2 (1979):24–35.

what remains permits us to say a great deal about the cultures of Israel and its neighbors and about how the people lived, worshiped, and went about their everyday lives.

The word "archaeology" in the phrase "archaeology and the Old Testament" or "biblical archaeology" has a very broad meaning, indeed, encompassing all or part of many discrete disciplines, each of which may shed light at points on the Old Testament as a historical, literary, or religious document. Some of the potentially informative areas, such as Mesopotamian studies, are themselves collections of disciplines and subdisciplines which may require a lifetime of study to master. Even within so small an area as Palestine, subdisciplines such as study of the Dead Sea Scrolls or of Hebrew epigraphy have evolved into separate specialties; one can be an expert in the scrolls, an "archaeological" subject, without ever having turned over a single clod of earth in an "archaeological" excavation. Since the purpose of the present volume is to explore the methods that "archaeologists" use when relating their finds to the Old Testament, we would have an impossible task were we to continue to use the word "archaeology" in the broad sense. Therefore, in Chapters II and IV we shall narrow our view to a single aspect of the relationship between "archaeology" and the Old Testament, namely, the excavation of materials in Palestine and the way they are used to illumine the cultural and historical environment in which the Hebrew scriptures were written. In Chapters III and V, we shall again be looking at some broader issues.

FOR FURTHER READING

The reader who wishes to investigate further the general impact of archaeology on the Bible will find summaries in the following:

Albright, William F. *The Archaeology of Palestine*. Gloucester, Mass.: P. Smith, 1971.

———. *From Stone Age to Christianity*. 2d ed. Garden City, N.Y.: Doubleday Anchor Books, 1957.

Cornfeld, Gaalyah. *Archaeology of the Bible: Book by Book*. London: A. & C. Black, 1977.

Finegan, Jack. *Light from the Ancient Past*. 2d ed. Princeton, N.J.: Princeton University Press, 1959.

Frank, Harry Thomas. *Bible, Archaeology, and Faith*. Nashville: Abingdon Press, 1971.

Franken, H. J., and C. A. Franken-Battershill. *A Primer of Old Testament Archaeology*. Leiden: E. J. Brill, 1963.

Gray, John. *Archaeology and the Old Testament World*. London: Nelson & Sons, 1962.

Kenyon, Kathleen M. *Archaeology in the Holy Land*. 4th ed. London: Ernest Benn; and New York: W. W. Norton, 1979.

————. *The Bible and Recent Archaeology*. London: British Museum Publications, 1978.

Kitchen, K. A. *The Bible in Its World*. Exeter: Paternoster Press, 1977.

Magnusson, Magnus. *BC: The Archaeology of the Bible Lands*. London: Bodley Head and British Broadcasting Corporation, 1977.

Paul, Shalom M. and William G. Dever, eds. *Biblical Archaeology*. Jerusalem: Keter Publishing House, 1974.

Price, Ira Maurice, Ovid R. Sellers, and E. Leslie Carlson. *The Monuments and the Old Testament*. Philadelphia: Judson Press, 1958.

Pritchard, James B. *Archaeology and the Old Testament*. Oxford: Oxford University Press, 1958.

Schoville, Keith N. *Biblical Archaeology in Focus*. Grand Rapids, Mich.: Baker Book House, 1978.

Wright, G. Ernest. *Biblical Archaeology*. rev. ed. London: Gerald Duckworth and Philadelphia: Westminster Press, 1962.

II

Basic Principles:
Stratigraphy and Typology

How do things get buried in the first place? This is a question which any archaeological lecturer soon learns to anticipate from an audience. The fact is that not all archaeological objects are buried. The Dead Sea Scrolls were found in jars in caves. Ancient inscriptions and graffiti survive carved into the living rock or scratched on the walls of tombs. In some cases campsites, walls, and even whole structures have survived for several millennia above ground in remote areas. Then there is material that once was buried but by one means or another has come to the surface. Modern plowing of ancient sites or the winter rains continually bring up small objects and pottery fragments. Far more destructive are the illicit diggers who either for gain or out of misguided enthusiasm rob tombs or plunder sites, forever destroying the context in which the object was preserved along with most of its historical meaning.

Most finds, however, are indeed buried or, to use the technical term, stratified; that is, they are found below the present surface of the ground in relationship to layers of earth that cover or contain them. Burial can occur in all sorts of ways. Trash and garbage thrown continually over a city wall will in time form deep trash heaps or middens. Some things are intentionally buried, such as the entrances to tombs. Others are buried by the natural processes of erosion or the accumulation and decay of vegetable matter. But by far the most numerous examples of stratification are the hundreds of mounds that dot the face of the Near East. In Palestine these mounds which contain the ruins of ancient cities are called tells, a word borrowed from Arabic, also current in its Hebrew form, tel.

Basically, the tell is a layer cake, albeit an enormous and complicated one, created by the accumulation of the remains of successive human occupation of the same site, sometimes over a period of thousands of years (Fig. 1). That the mounds on which cities were situated were

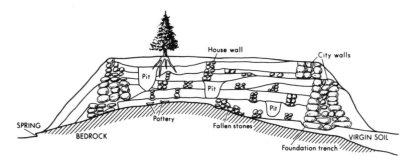

FIG. 1. SECTION THROUGH A SMALL TELL

different from ordinary hills was known already to the biblical writers: Deut. 13:16 directs the Israelites to destroy utterly any city that permits apostasy from Yahweh and to make it "a tell forever." Tells are in fact huge human artifacts, artificial hills, every stone of which has been carried there by design. Thus an ancient mound is not simply a repository of interesting objects; it is an interesting object in its own right and, as we shall see, has come to be treated more as such in recent years.

The Formation of the Mound

Let us rehearse the process that produces the typical tell. The first inhabitants would be drawn to the site by some natural advantage it possessed. Until the invention of cisterns, Palestine's dry summer season required that every settlement be near some permanent water source—a stream that flows year round (of which there are few in Palestine), a spring, or a well. In the vicinity of the spring or water supply there needed to be enough terrain sufficiently level or that could be terraced so that houses could be built. Preferable would be a hill or rise with enough elevation to let the inhabitants size up approaching strangers from a distance, for such a height could be more easily defended. Furthermore, the site needed some economic base—farming, grazing, trading, or even government support, such as the city of Samaria which the kings of Israel created as their capital.

The first settlers would build their houses and other buildings on the exposed bedrock or on virgin soil, using building techniques that have survived until the present day in the poorer and more remote areas of the country. The major materials, to be had for the taking,

13

were fieldstone and mudbrick, used in various combinations. Typically, at least in the hill country, stone foundations would simply be laid on the bare rock or soil. Or the settlers might first outline the plan of the building by digging a shallow trench in which to lay the foundation—one, two, or more rows of stones wide, and one or more courses high. Usually the builders would use the stones just as they came from the fields, without dressing. Although the stones would probably be laid with mud mortar in order to seal out the weather and to discourage pests, the strength and solidity of the foundation depended upon stone-to-stone contact, a difficult trick to achieve with stones of irregular shape, as anyone who has attempted to imitate these building techniques can attest.

Depending on current fashion and on the materials at hand, stone might also be used for the walls. More often, however, they would be of sundried mudbrick, today widely known as adobe, and still the major building material in much of the world. Clay and straw are kneaded together (Exod. 5:6–7), pressed into molds, and tipped out to dry in the sun. The bricks of the period of the Israelite monarchy were often rectangular, roughly 24 by 16 inches and 5 or 6 inches thick. Mudbrick can be quite satisfactory as a building material, but it must be diligently replastered and maintained against the ravages of weather or it will swiftly decay.

As for the roofs of houses, they were generally flat and made of timbers that supported thick layers of mud and straw or reeds pressed together, sometimes by stone roof-rollers. Sufficiently thick, such a layer would keep out the weather but, like the walls, demanded constant attention and repair.

The interior decor would vary according to current style and the wealth of the owner. Generally the floors would be of beaten earth; they were no doubt covered in the living quarters by mats and rugs. If more elegance or impermeability to water was desired, the surfaces could be plastered, a treatment which was often extended to the walls as well. When a tougher flooring was needed or one that the winter rains could not turn to mud, then cobblestones or flagstones were the answer. Stone and clay also provided the material for all the domestic and industrial facilities—hearths, bins, ovens, wine vats, jar-supports, worktables, and so on.

If such a building were in use for any length of time, it would usually need repair or alteration. Floors would need replastering; sometimes a section dug through such a floor will reveal a half-dozen or more layers of repair. Doorways were blocked up and new ones opened. Rooms were added or subdivided. Refuse or storage pits were dug and re-

filled. But finally at some stage, the building would come to an end—
by violence, intentional demolition, or neglect—and the growth of the
mound would begin.

Forces of destruction were all too numerous in the ancient world:
accidental fire, fire set by brigands or conquering armies, earthquake,
and even torrential rain. Let us take the example of a conquest and
total destruction by fire, the sort which gives archaeologists such per-
verse delight because it brings to a clear end one period of occupation
of the site and covers everything with a thick layer of ashes and debris.
Usually the conquerors would first loot the settlement of its valuables,
although sometimes overlooking hidden treasure and, of course, caring
nothing for the common pottery which they would smash and scatter
about in the search, thereby giving essential data, as we shall see, to
the archaeologist. If they wanted to make sure that the devastation
would be complete, they might pull out beams and roof supports before
setting fire to everything combustible (see 2 Chron. 34:11; Ezra 6:11).
Since we rarely find human remains in such destruction levels, we must
assume that the slain were either buried or cast uninterred outside the
city (see Jer. 16:4). The survivors would either flee into the country-
side or, if captured, be sold into slavery. Living a peaceful and pros-
perous life into old age could not be taken for granted in the ancient
world.

As for the site, it would be a jumble of smoking ruins and toppled
walls. Any of a number of things might now happen: stragglers could
return and camp out in the rubble while trying to rebuild; the site
might be abandoned for a year or for a thousand years; it might never
be reinhabited. But let us suppose that new settlers arrive a few years
after the period of warfare that destroyed the original village. In the
meantime, the site has been at the mercy of the elements, particularly
the powerful winter rains. Under their pelting the broken mudbrick
turns once again into mud which erodes, filling the low spots. The rains
might also cut deep gulleys into the debris or undermine walls still
standing so that they too collapse. It would not take many rainy seasons until there remained little evidence of prior human presence—a
stone wall here, a stump of stubborn mudbrick there. The surfaces on
which the prior inhabitants lived out their lives would now be buried
a few inches or a few feet under the debris.

When the new settlers surveyed the area, they would be drawn to
the spot of the previous habitation by the same factors that had made
it desirable in the first place: its access to water, visibility, strategic
importance, and so on. Moreover, the leveled ruins would have added
to the height and defensibility of the site. The exposed stones of the old

15

walls were ready sources of building stone of the proper size; and by a little digging, what archaeologists call "robbing," still more could be uncovered. The people would pull down any remaining mudbrick walls, perhaps using the debris to level uneven places and to refill their own robber pits, covering the earlier surfaces yet more deeply. They would need fresh clay and additional stone, which they would haul in from the fields, thus adding to the total mass of the mound. Their work done, they would settle down to life in their new village until the process would be triggered again by the next destruction, perhaps an earthquake which can have an unbelievably devastating effect on mudbrick structures. Then the cycle would begin all over, eventually producing stratum upon stratum of debris, each of which may have subphases in which individual buildings were purposely remodeled or accidentally destroyed and rebuilt. The site of Gezer, for example, has twenty-six identifiable strata plus many subphases, covering a period of more than three thousand years.

The process of mound formation is far more complicated than this schematic reconstruction indicates; indeed it will be as infinitely varied as a combination of human and natural forces can produce. The surface of the mound at any period of its growth may be quite level or quite irregular. Some buildings may suffer destruction while others are undisturbed. Earlier strata may be entirely scraped off, creating the illusion of a gap in the occupational history. Erosion may gulley the mound, carrying materials downslope from one stratum to be mixed with materials of an earlier stratum. The foundations of later periods, particularly heavy fortification systems, may cut through many earlier layers or they may be founded outside the contemporary perimeter of the mound on the same bedrock on which the earliest houses were built. Two disturbances which perpetrate particular mischief call for special mention: pits and fills.

Pits

To the everlasting frustration of archaeologists, the ancients dug pits with inexhaustible zeal—refuse pits, storage pits, robber pits—sometimes of astonishing size. The memory of one distressing example from our excavations at the site of Gezer is still painfully fresh. In the group of squares on the top of the mound we called Field VI we uncovered part of what had clearly been an imposing building of the fourteenth century B.C., the Amarna age in Palestine in which Gezer had played so important a role. However, these buildings had been turned into Swiss cheese by pitters of a hundred or so years later who had driven huge holes through this stratum and everything under it down to bedrock.

Massive pitting on this scale will be easily detectable by a skilled archaeologist. Most pits dug by the ancients, however, were smaller and more varied in their history; and it is this variety that will produce such complications for the future digger. The reason for this is simple: pits, small or large, were eventually filled in again, and the filling could come from anywhere. It could be the debris originally dug from the pit. It could be refuse discarded into the pit over a long period. It could be fill brought from elsewhere on the site. It could be the result of slow erosion into the pit. Thus, a pit not only pierces the earlier layers in which it was dug, but it introduces into them whatever was used to refill the pit, which can be almost anything from a wide chronological range. Since the pit fill can be nearly indistinguishable in appearance from the earth of the layers into which it was dug, the chance for mixture in excavating is high and the consequences are serious.

Let us illustrate by two examples, one analogical and one archaeological. Suppose a library shelf contained a set of forty volumes on science published in 1840 bound identically in dark brown. One day a reader removes Vol. XII (analogous to digging a pit) and replaces it with a book from a later edition of the set, nearly identical in shape and color, but published in 1910. A casual observer would see nothing amiss; the set would appear to be intact. Let us assume that someone proceeds to use the set to write a description of the state of science in 1840 but fails to notice the publication date of Vol. XII. To the extent that the researcher made use of Vol. XII, the conclusions would be distorted, because that volume in fact represents the science of 1910, not 1840.

In Fig. 2 we have an archaeological case. Let us suppose that Pit D was dug in the eighth century B.C. down into a stratum of the tenth century and was filled in with rubbish from the eighth century. Since pits tend to bottom out on surfaces, probably because the extra degree of hardness of the surface discouraged the original pitters, a broken pot from the eighth century at the bottom of the pit has ended up resting on a tenth-century surface. If the excavators are not alert to the presence of pits, they will assume that the eighth-century pot belongs with Stratum A and thus will try to date the surface to the eighth century instead of the tenth. (The end of a stratum must be dated by the latest material found in it.) Even more mischievous, the excavators will publish the material from Pit D along with other pottery, let us say, from

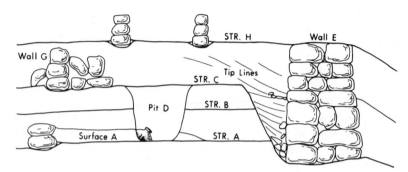

FIG. 2. TYPICAL PIT AND FILL

Surface A; and since the latest material is from the eighth century, they will try to argue that the other forms found on Surface A must also be from the eighth century. The annals of Palestinian archaeology unfortunately are full of cases in which this sort of thing has happened, thus introducing confusion that could have been avoided by greater awareness of the presence of pits.

Fills

Fills create similar problems.[1] Fig. 2 again provides an obvious example. At the end of Stratum C there was no violent destruction. Instead the occupants decided to build a large city wall, Wall E, and to raise the height of the mound in that area for improved defensibility. First they cut through the surfaces of Strata C, B, and A (another pit!) to prepare a huge foundation trench to seat the new defense wall. Then they demolished the structures of Stratum C, for example Wall G, and brought in fill to cover the entire area and to bring the mound up to the level of the top of the foundation of Wall E, whereon they laid the stone foundations for the new buildings of Stratum H. The fill was dug up from who knows where and could contain material from off the mound as well as from all periods of the mound's history down to and including the beginning of Stratum H. If, for example, the fill were dug up from one single place, it might be full of consistent pottery of the tenth century B.C., even though Stratum C is eighth century, thus inverting the stratification from the point of view of the objects in the layer. A careless archaeologist might assume that since the fill is full of tenth-century pottery, Wall E and Stratum H must therefore be

1. See G. Ernest Wright, "Archaeological Fills and Strata," *BA* 25 (1962):34–40.

dated to the tenth century. The example presented here may make the problem of fills appear simple, but let me cite another (and more embarrassing!) example.

Our first project at Gezer was a long narrow stratigraphic trench designed to provide us with a section through the debris of the mound at its deepest point as well as across the fortification systems. At the lower end of the trench we soon uncovered an enormous stone tower some 15.6 meters (over 50 ft.) across, the largest single-phase stone structure ever discovered in Palestine. On top of this tower toward its inner side, we found several curious stone platforms for which no clear purpose was ever discerned. Under these platforms and on top of the huge stones of the tower itself was a thin layer of soil which contained a number of sherds of small bowls with a bright-red inner rim, a type which could be dated to about 1800 B.C. There was nothing of a later period. Consequently, we concluded that the tower itself should be dated to about 1800 B.C. and published this judgment in several early reports. In later seasons, however, indisputable evidence accumulated for a much later date for the building of the tower, somewhere around 1600 B.C. How, then, to explain the presence of the earlier sherds on *top* of the wall, obviously placed there after the wall's construction, some 200 years later? Clearly it was fill. After the tower was finished, the builders carted in some debris from elsewhere on the mound in which by chance all the sherds were from around 1800 B.C.; and on this layer of early debris, they built those strange platforms. And so we were forced to retract our previously published date for the tower and to redate it some 200 years later.[2]

The Role of the City Wall

One final factor in the process of mound-building calls for mention, namely the role of the city wall. Unwalled settlements did not become mounds; erosion eventually leveled the entire site. For a tell to form, the settlement had to have a defense wall around the perimeter. These walls would generally be massive versions of the house walls already described, namely a mudbrick superstructure seated on a solid stone foundation (see Wall E in Fig. 2). The superstructure eventually decays and erodes down the slope of the mound; but the stone foundations remain in place and act as a terrace wall, preventing the debris on the top of the tell from being washed away. The result is a hill with a flat top, a "tell-tale" shape which the sharp-eyed visitor to the mod-

2. William G. Dever, H. Darrell Lance, and G. Ernest Wright, *Gezer I: Preliminary Report of the 1964–66 Seasons* (Jerusalem: Hebrew Union College Biblical and Archaeological School, 1970), p. 42 and n. 5.

ern Near East soon learns to distinguish from the rounder contours of the natural hills.

If it is now clear what a tell is and how it grows, it should also be clear that each tell is unique: the stratification can be quite simple, for example, large level buildings covered by thick homogeneous destruction debris. Or it can be frustratingly complex—pitted, eroded, leveled, terraced, trenched, filled, and pitted again until the original sequence is virtually impossible to reconstruct. Nevertheless, what we have learned thus far may be fairly simply summarized.

1. A mound is a combination of architectural or living levels and the earth layers which overlie, underlie, or interrupt them. Although the architectural levels or strata will naturally be of greatest interest, only by reconstructing the story of the debris layers can those architectural elements be put in proper relation to each other and to the other material remains. Even in the absence of architecture the debris layers themselves contain important information that the archaeologist can recover. The entire mound is a human artifact with a unique story; the debris layers are as much a part of that story as the architecture.

2. A mound is a three-dimensional jigsaw puzzle, composed of lenses and layers of earth lying on or around or under remains of architecture or other traces of human occupation. Some pieces are enormous, such as the Gezer tower mentioned above; some are so tiny as to be stratigraphically meaningless, such as each separate basket of earth poured in to create the fill in Fig. 2. True, to think of a mound as composed of separate pieces is to some extent a logical construct, a scheme which the archaeologist imposes. In real life, both when the mound was being formed and when one attempts to disassemble it, things are much less clear. Nevertheless, the theory is correct; from the houses built by the first settlers on bedrock to the candy wrapper dropped by yesterday's tourist, the mound was formed piece by discrete piece.

3. The individual elements of the mound, the pieces of the three-dimensional jigsaw puzzle, were put in place sequentially; each piece came to its present location either before or after or simultaneously with the piece next to it. Two major factors affect the way the pieces interrelate: the force of gravity and human activity. (As an example of a minor factor, one might cite the complications introduced by burrowing animals.) Gravity constantly works to flatten the mound. Moreover, it decrees that every wall or installation was originally built by someone standing on a surface. That surface may later have been cut away or removed, but not once in all Palestine's many mounds did

someone build a wall in midair. (Such a denial may seem superfluous, but more than one frustrated stratigrapher has been nearly convinced of the opposite.) At every moment of the mound's existence, there was a surface, however transitory or humble, everywhere over the entire mound, not just within houses or buildings. If a surface ended or was cut, it was cut by something creating another surface in the process.

The second factor, the human one, is unpredictable, inventive, and somewhat capricious. Nevertheless, human activity, constructive or destructive, is also bound by the law of gravity and must proceed one piece at a time, always in relationship to something already in place—removing it, covering it, modifying it, but never vertically separated from it. The implication of all this is clear: careful observation of structures and layers can reveal a relative sequence based on the simple principle that the one on top is necessarily younger than the one underneath. The sequence in time is certain; the interval, however, may be a matter of minutes or of centuries.

4. The stratification of many mounds is so complex that the process of disassembly of the three-dimensional jigsaw puzzle is an ideal that cannot be achieved in reality by any method thus far contrived. Or, to put it another way, the reconstructed stratigraphy of a mound will correlate to the actual fact by a greater or lesser percentage, but the correlation will be far short of 100 percent. There are simply too many unpredictable and, for all practical purposes, uncontrollable variables. For example, decayed mudbrick is often so full of clay that a few swipes of a trowel can produce a hard earthen "surface" almost at will; and the actual surface on which the debris fell may not be recognized as such when it is finally reached. By contrast, an eager worker can scrape and clean an earthen surface so thoroughly that it vanishes completely before it is properly described and recorded. In short, the all-important division into coherent pieces is often not achieved exactly, because of both the difficulty of the problem and the fallibility of the excavator.

This human factor is one of the variables that is most difficult to control. Some members of an excavation staff will have a natural feel for stratification; others of equal intelligence will find it bewildering. Some will have an eye for soil, for gradations in color and hardness; to others it will all seem the same. Some dig directors will keep a tight rein on their staff; others will allow carelessness or will try to oversee so many operations that proper supervision is impossible. The actual work of excavating is performed by hired laborers or volunteers, some of whom will be conscientious, industrious, alert, and experienced; but others will be lazy, distracted, bored, and insufficiently trained. Even the weather makes a difference; the context of a minor object found in the cool of the morning may receive more adequate attention than a major find when the sun is broiling hot, the excavators are tired, and the lunch bell is ringing. In short, excavation is not a science and never will be, both because the entity being excavated is too complex ever to be understood fully and because the humanity of the excavator and the unfavorable conditions in which most excavation has to be carried out inevitably produce error, distortion, and misinterpretation.

The Methods of Excavation

In response to the difficulties of untangling the stratification of tells, modern Palestinian archaeology has developed or adopted several methods and concepts to maximize the percentage of accurate information produced by an excavation. These ideas are embodied in a vast lore of practical digging technique which, however, we shall illustrate only in passing. Instead, we shall concentrate on the major concepts a reader needs to understand in order to interpret primary archaeological reports and to evaluate them critically.[3]

The Locus

Let us suppose that you, the reader, are an archaeologist standing atop a mound which you are going to dig. You know that under your feet lie hundreds, perhaps thousands, of years of history in the form of a complicated three-dimensional jigsaw puzzle, many of the pieces stuck tightly together and ready to defy your best attempt to separate them cleanly. Your overall goal, which will need repetition as you proceed lest it be drowned in a sea of secondary issues, is to learn about the people whose labor built this mound and, as far as possible, to reconstruct their lives, history, and environment stratum by stratum. To do this successfully, you must try to unstack the pieces of the puzzle in the exact reverse order of the way that human industry and the force of gravity deposited them. In most of the pieces you will find data— pottery, artifacts, environmental evidence such as bones, seeds, and pollen—which you will then study and use to reconstruct on paper the story of what you find.

You will be relieved to know that good archaeological method is fundamentally the systematic application of intelligent common sense to the peculiar problems of stratification. True, there is a vast amount

3. For a detailed discussion of the concepts and procedures discussed in the following pages, see William G. Dever and H. Darrell Lance, eds., *A Manual of Field Excavation* (New York: Hebrew Union College–Jewish Institute of Religion, 1978).

of practical wisdom which has been built up through collective experience as well as many technical scientific procedures one ignores at one's peril; but in the last analysis there is no single approach that will always in every situation guarantee the recovery of the information you are seeking. If a mound were the proverbial cat, there would be more than one good way to skin it. But there are many more bad ways to do it, and this nod to relativism should not be construed as the archaeological equivalent of the satirical adage, "It doesn't matter what you believe so long as you are sincere." How you dig matters a great deal and for an obvious reason: archaeology is a nonrepeatable discipline. Once a particular part of a mound has been excavated, no one will ever be able to excavate that exact spot again. To excavate is to destroy. Those who dig an ancient site must justify themselves before all human history, past and future, that they excavated with all the care that befits the solemnity of the task. But lest the vision of standing in the dock before all humanity dissuade you utterly, be assured that the combination of accumulated experience plus good sense can provide sufficient guidance.

For example, as you contemplate the unbroken surface of your mound, you realize that before you can slice into the three-dimensional jigsaw puzzle on which you stand, you need a clear and logical way to conceptualize and process what you will find. First of all, unless you excavate an entire mound at once—a task so daunting that it is almost never attempted—you will be sectioning, that is, cutting down vertically, through many of the pieces of the puzzle, leaving parts of them unexcavated. Although you will be removing in their entirety some of the pieces of the puzzle, others will be sliced through in an arbitrary and misleading way. But the awareness of this fact will prevent you from pressing your evidence too hard, making general conclusions that may be unwarranted.

In order to handle the whole or partial pieces of the puzzle as you find them, you will need some concept sufficiently inclusive to apply to everything that you encounter, earth layer and architecture alike. In the excavations of Gezer, we used the word "locus" for this concept (a word which the reader should be aware is used by different archaeologists to mean different things); but the specific term is irrelevant so long as the concept is clear. A locus as defined at Gezer is the smallest coherent unit of stratigraphy, that is, the smallest significant piece of the puzzle—a consistent layer, the prepared surface on which the layer rested or on which the destruction debris fell, the fill that was brought in to provide a smooth base on which to lay the surface, each wall of a house, each successive repair of a wall, a group of smashed vessels on

23

a surface, the contents of a pit, the stone lining of a pit that separated the contents from the layers into which the pit was dug, and so on. A locus may be large—for example, the huge single-phase stone tower from Gezer mentioned above—or it may be small—a patch of cobbles on an earthen floor. Each locus or piece of the puzzle needs to be identified permanently by a system of numbering so that it can be referred to and identified in plans, sections, and descriptions. In Fig. 3A and B, the elements have been labeled according to the Gezer system. Sometimes in the confusion of actual excavation, the same locus may be assigned more than one number; but this is easily resolved when the total picture becomes clear. The crucial point is that no piece of the puzzle be left floating, as it were, unassigned to a locus. The way each piece is isolated and identified, the terminology involved, and the clarity of the results will vary from excavator to excavator.

The Recording System

Now supplied with a clear concept of the piece of the mound and a name for it, you may suppose you are ready at last to begin digging. Alas, not quite. Before you can remove a single clod of earth, you must have a complete system ready to record what you find and in what context. Archaeology, as already mentioned, is a nonrepeatable discipline. Once something is excavated it cannot be put back for another more careful go at it. When the excavation is finished, all that remains are the artifacts or materials that have been kept and stored away, the records on paper and film, and a hole in the ground. Unless there is some way to reconstruct on paper the original relationship of the groups of materials that have been preserved, they lose all historical value and become mere antique curios. Whatever system of recording is used—and there are many possibilities so long as they are thorough, workable, and complete—must be in place before digging begins, just as an operating room in a hospital must contain equipment to meet all contingencies before the first incision in even the most routine operation. As you excavate, you must be able to transfer your findings immediately into the records. Recording is a continuous process; and if it fails at any point, the bit of information affected may be irretrievably lost. It is the rare excavator who has not known the awful moment when his or her workers have just carried out an order to dismantle some wall or to remove a plaster floor, only to have the photographer appear at the edge of the trench to inquire, "Where is the thing you wanted me to photograph?" What Lady Macbeth observed of murder is true also of archaeology: "What's done cannot be undone."

This is not the place even to outline all the elements of a full recording system, but some understanding of what is involved is necessary for a critical reading of archaeological reports. Quite simply, the recording system must be able to handle all of the complexities of a tell as they are uncovered. Every layer of earth or bucket of pottery, every bead or bangle, every sample of bone or seed, each wall, surface, oven, bin, every drawing or photograph must slide smoothly into a ready niche in the recording system so that someone can reconstruct the progress of excavation, step by step, in order to determine the proper relationship among finds. Not all of this information will be useful; even less will ultimately be published. But unless the system has a fine mesh, there is no guarantee that it will catch some small datum which seems trivial at the time but may turn out to be crucial. In recent years, excavation projects have become much more self-conscious and intentional in regard to their recording systems; and the newer dig reports often include a systematic explanation of their procedures so that the reader can make a considered judgment about their thoroughness and adequacy.[4]

Given the three-dimensional nature of a tell, a major requirement of any recording system is to provide orientation in space. Typically, the horizontal dimension is furnished by a surveyor who prepares a contour map of the site on which a grid of squares is imposed, often but not always oriented to the compass. Once this is done, any area of excavation or any piece of architecture within an area can be related two-dimensionally to everything else. The third dimension is also provided by the surveyor, at least in absolute terms. (In vertical orientation it is often the relative relationship that is more important, and we shall return to this later.) Some point is chosen, one that will not be removed during the digging, to serve as a permanent reference in elevation. Preferably this point is provided by the national survey of the country where the excavation is to take place, expressed as an absolute datum above sea level. These principles are not difficult, and a single illustration may suffice.

Fig. 3B is the ground-plan of an area 3 by 5 meters in size. (Except in very early British or American excavations, all archaeologists use the metric system.) Because the grid which determined the placement of the square was fixed by the compass, the architecture found in the area

4. E.g., Yohanan Aharoni et al., "Methods of Recording and Documentation," *Beer-sheba I: Excavations at Tel Beer-sheba, 1969–71 Seasons*, ed. Yohanan Aharoni (Tel Aviv: Tel Aviv Institute of Archaeology, 1973), pp. 119–32; William G. Dever, H. Darrell Lance, G. Ernest Wright, *Gezer I: Preliminary Report of the 1964–66 Seasons* (Jerusalem: Hebrew Union College Biblical and Archaeological School, 1970), pp. 9–13; H. J. Franken, *Excavations at Tell Deir 'Allā I: A Stratigraphical and Analytical Study of the Early Iron Age Pottery* (Leiden: E. J. Brill, 1969), pp. 15–19.

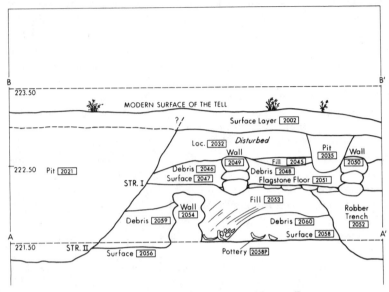

FIG. 3. (A) SECTION DRAWING OF NORTH BALK

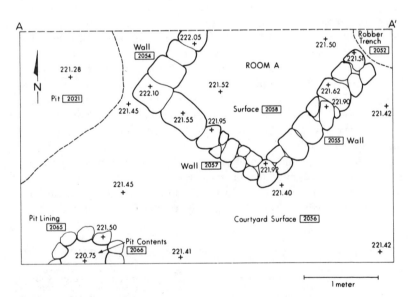

FIG. 3. (B) PLAN OF STRATUM II

will often, as in this case, be oriented diagonally. Fig. 3B represents a scale drawing of the exposed part of a house prepared by the dig draftsman. If the drawing was well done, each stone of the drawing should be recognizable in a photograph of the same house. In the lower left corner is the rim of a partially exposed pit that was dug into the courtyard of the house. Without too much difficulty, the reader, by noticing the scale, can reconstruct the proportions and appearance of the plan of the original building and courtyard.

It is more difficult to show the third dimension. Photographs can help, and archaeological publications make as much use of them as publication budgets allow. But on two-dimensional drawings the only way to give a sense of depth is by the use of reduced levels plotted on the plan. Starting from the preestablished vertical reference point, the surveyor can determine the relative height of any point on the mound by the use of a theodolite and leveling rod. When the draftsman has finished drawing the walls and plotting the surface of a stratum, reduced levels are taken on a series of points which can be compared to give some sense of the relative heights of the spots so marked. Thus, in looking at Fig. 3B we see that the absolute elevation above sea level of Surface 2056 is 221.40 to 221.45 meters. (The relationship to sea level per se is, of course, archaeologically meaningless; sea level is simply the reference point in this case.) The figure 221.92 on the corner of Walls 2055 and 2057 tells us that the topmost surviving course of stones at this corner is 52 centimeters above adjacent Surface 2056 (221.40 subtracted from 221.92). As we trace the levels of Wall 2055 along its length to the northeast, we learn that the wall survives at the same approximate height for a meter or so but then becomes more ruined as it approaches the corner of the area. The levels step down to 221.62 and then 221.51 meters, roughly the same as the floor of Room A, which suggests that the wall originally extended farther but has been robbed out. Tracing Wall 2057 to the northwest away from the corner, we again detect a difference in levels, this time quite abrupt. The large stone in this wall has a level of only 221.55 meters, some 40 cm. below the stone on one side and 55 cm. below the corner with Wall 2054. Thus, we may suppose that this stone represents the threshold of a doorway from the house into the courtyard. The typical archaeological plan will have many such levels on it, permitting us in our imagination to add the third dimension to a two-dimensional plan.

Although levels are essential to show the third dimension of plans, they are nearly meaningless when it comes to putting debris layers and the artifacts found in or between them into the third dimension. Let us assume, for example, that in excavating Room A of Fig. 3B, you find

27

two groups of broken pottery on the floor, one group at the north edge of the excavated area, next to Wall 2054, and the other, also along the north edge of the area but farther to the east (right in the figure). If you were to try to indicate the third dimension of the find spot of these two groups of pottery by the use of levels, your records would indicate the same information for both since both were found at the level of Surface 2058. But because you were digging carefully, separating each piece of the mound (what we shall hereafter consistently call a locus) from those next to it, you were able to determine that the pottery up against Wall 2054 was part of a debris layer, a fill, which was thrown into the ruins of the house sometime after the house was destroyed. This means that the pottery in the fill dates to the time the fill was put in or some time before, not to the time of the destruction of the house. The pottery found on Surface 2058 a bit farther to the east, however, *was* part of the destruction debris of the house and should be determinative in dating that destruction. How, then, do you demonstrate this finding to skeptical colleagues who will want to conclude that, since both groups of pottery were found at the same level and on Surface 2058, they are contemporary? The answer is provided by the second way that archaeologists have of recording vertical relationships, namely the measured section.

A section in the archaeological sense is a cut through something, often made to reveal its internal structure. Usually it is vertical. A section through a plaster floor can reveal how thick the plaster is, on what it was laid, how many times it was repaired, and so on. A section through an entire mound or part of it would look like Fig. 1 or 2. Every time the excavator digs a hole, he or she has the chance to see something in section. Archaeologists have learned to turn necessity into virtue and have made the interpretation and recording of sections their most useful tool for analyzing and demonstrating vertical relationships.

The sides of the area being excavated provide the major sections. For the purposes of order and control, digging normally goes on within the bounds of a limited area, usually square (5 by 5 meters is the most common size) or rectangular, depending on terrain, project goals, and many other factors. If another area is opened immediately adjacent, then a space, usually a meter in width, is left unexcavated between the areas, forming a visible grid as the excavation deepens. These unexcavated dividers are called balks ("baulk" in British spelling), and the vertical faces of the balks provide the needed sections. If the balks are kept carefully trimmed and smoothed, not only will they provide a check on the correct separation of debris layers in the excavation process, but also they can frequently yield additional information that would otherwise be missed.

Fig. 3A is a drawing of the north balk of the area being excavated in Fig. 3B. The section drawing is printed above the plan so that you may see that the features at the north edge of the plan also enter the balk, such as Wall 2054, Pit 2021, and Robber Trench 2052. The plan and the section drawing together represent the ground-plan and the north side of the excavated area. Just as each locus is numbered in the drawing, so in the actual balk, each feature would be marked by tags nailed in for easy reference. Line A–A' is the same in each drawing. Let us look at Fig. 3A to see what it can tell us.

The primary purpose of a section drawing is to record the relationship of the loci as they originated in the process of the mound's formation. With the addition of datum points, represented by the dotted lines A–A' and B–B', we can also show absolute levels for ease of correlation with plans. Looking at the section, we could argue for the following sequence of events: The lowest surfaces, 2056 in the courtyard and 2058 inside the house, and Wall 2054 are obviously the earliest elements; the relationship between the wall and the surfaces cannot be determined until more digging is done. Debris 2059 slopes up to and adheres to the stones of Wall 2054, which shows that Wall 2054 existed before Debris 2059. Otherwise there would be traces of a trench through Debris 2059 into which Wall 2054 was placed. We cannot tell how long Wall 2054 was in place before Debris 2059 arrived; sections by themselves give only relative dates. Likewise, we cannot know if Debris 2059 and 2060 came into being simultaneously or in some other sequence. Without other information, we would probably conclude that they originated together since they both rest on contemporary surfaces with no sign of a build-up of occupation debris on either surface. This inference would be strengthened if Debris 2059 and 2060 were similar in composition, for example, if both contained the bits of charred wood and partially burned mudbrick that are typical of a destruction by fire. Since Debris 2060 covers restorable pieces of pottery (Locus 2058P) on Surface 2058, we may conclude that it most probably represents a sudden destruction. Apparently new settlers rebuilt within a short time; the debris of Locus 2060 did not have time to erode and form a layer of silt running up to Wall 2054. In order to cover over the destruction debris to provide a surface for the buildings of the new stratum, the settlers dumped in a quantity of fill, Locus 2053. In digging elsewhere on the mound for the fill material, they came across a large storage jar from a stratum of 200 years earlier which was broken and thus of no use to them. So they threw it into the ruins where it came to rest on Surface 2058 next to Wall 2054. In any case, the new inhabitants leveled off the area and prepared to build.

At this juncture, having failed to plan ahead, the settlers realized they needed foundation stone and so were forced to dig a robber trench through their own Fill 2053, Debris 2060, and Surface 2058 to lay bare the stones of Wall 2055. Perhaps some stones of Wall 2055 were still protruding above the surface after they had finished filling while Wall 2054 had been covered and forgotten. At any rate, after refilling their own robber trench, Locus 2052, they then proceeded to build the structures of the next stratum, Walls 2049, 2050, and Flagstone Floor 2051. And the process repeated itself.

As eloquent as a section drawing can be, one might object that it represents the realities only of one single plane through the mound. The position of that plane is determined by the grid which may have no relationship to the layout of the strata. Moreover, what about the layers that were dug in the middle of the area and never reached the main balk? Or, from another point of view, how can one have any confidence that just a few centimeters inside the balk, the picture might not be quite different? One can make several responses.

Some of these problems have simple practical solutions. For example, temporary cross-balks can be used to tie isolated areas or awkwardly placed elements of architecture into the main sections. Moreover, if the digging proceeds carefully by debris layers, the excavator can indicate in words the relationship between loci so that eventually contact is made with a main section. Let us assume, for example, that in excavating the corner formed by Walls 2057 and 2055 in Room A of Fig. 3B you found a distinct layer of soft yellowish soil from which several important objects were recovered. This locus to which the number 2061 was assigned was localized in the one corner, a sort of bank that sloped down and away from the walls and disappeared before reaching the north balk. Since you will want to discuss the objects found in this locus, you need to give the readers of your report a clear idea of its stratigraphic situation. This you could do by describing it in terms of loci which do reach the north section (Fig. 3A), saying, for example, that Locus 2061 was a bank of yellowish soil found on top of Locus 2060 and under Locus 2053. Since both of these loci are represented in the drawing of the north balk, it is clear that stratigraphically Locus 2061 is later than 2060 and earlier than 2053.

As for the objection that a section represents the stratigraphy only in a single plane and does not record the situation even a few centimeters inside the balk, one can only respond that all sampling techniques are subject to statistical error. The question is not whether a recording technique provides 100 percent accuracy; such a goal is utopian. Rather, the proper question is whether there is any other approach that would decrease the error more efficiently. Or, to put it another way, if the choice is between a partial and limited record on the one hand and no record at all on the other, it should be self-evident that something is better than nothing. Even if what a section shows is only partial, it is nevertheless real. A keen observer who spends a month in Paris may not be able to generalize about all of French culture, but he or she should be able to make some valid observations about Paris.

Perhaps the major argument for recording and publishing measured sections, that is, sections that have been drawn to scale, is that they prove that the excavator has in fact examined, analyzed, and made stratigraphic sense out of the work *in the field*. If the excavator cannot come to defensible conclusions in the field, the chances are far less that he or she will succeed in a study, surrounded only by photographs and written records. In those instances when even the excavator in the field cannot make plausible sense of the stratification, then the one who uses the published reports is forewarned not to base conclusions too heavily on evidence from the muddled loci.

Some have argued that drawn sections which represent only the opinion of the excavator are too subjective.[5] But surely it is the archaeologist in the field who has the best opportunity that will ever exist to understand and describe the stratigraphic situation. Being forced to draw sections that one must defend before one's colleagues compels the excavator to analyze the stratification with a rigor that no other method can replicate.[6]

The proof of any recording system comes after the results of the excavation have been published, for it is in the published form that the results will pass on to posterity. If the publication is unclear, incomplete, or confusing, then the use of the published materials must be proportionately cautious, qualified, and circumspect. The acid test of any final archaeological report is simple: Does it allow the reader to put the published find, be it potsherd or architectural complex, back into the stratigraphic context in which it was found, *working from the published evidence*? Or, to put it differently, can the reconstruction of the original stratification be based on data or must it be based on the word of the excavator? Excavators are fallible human beings; and their

5. Yohanan Aharoni, "Remarks on the 'Israeli' Method of Excavation (English summary)," *EI* 11 (1973):23*.
6. For an eloquent defense of the necessity of making and publishing measured sections as part of the recording system, see William G. Dever, "Two Approaches to Archaeological Method—The Architectural and the Stratigraphic," *EI* 11 (1973):1*–8*.

conclusions need to be tested by the data, which they themselves must provide in their publications. Moreover, future researchers will want to ask questions of dig reports that did not occur to the excavator; unless data are published fully, further research will be frustrated.

Let us illustrate these points by returning to Fig. 3A and B, which represent the area you have excavated and recorded at your site, which we shall assume is located within the bounds of ancient Judah. Suppose that someone wished to study the archaeological evidence for foreign influence on Judah in the period of the late monarchy. We shall assume for the sake of simplicity that the researcher is sufficiently versed in the Iron-Age cultures of the region to be able to recognize those objects that reveal a non-Israelite influence. A first step would be to search the pages of the drawings and photographs as well as the text of published dig reports for evidence—figurines, glyptic art (seals and seal impressions), amulets, imported pottery, and other objects. Let us suppose that the researcher found in your publication five such objects from the area depicted in Fig. 3A and B. These five objects came from the following loci: Surface 2058, Debris 2061, Robber Trench 2052, Debris 2048, and Pit 2021. Next, the researcher will want to know the date of the objects; for to demonstrate patterns of development, of increasing or decreasing influence, one must be able to date the evidence with some precision. We shall assume that you, the excavator, were able to demonstrate convincingly that Stratum II was destroyed in the eighth century B.C. and Stratum I in the early sixth century. The researcher, therefore, will want to know where these five loci are located stratigraphically in relation to these dated strata and will search the plans, sections, and verbal text of your report for answers.

Four of the five loci in question were sectioned by the north balk and hence are represented in Fig. 3A. The researcher will see immediately from the stratigraphy that the object found in Pit 2021 is impossible to date. The pit was obviously dug sometime after the destruction of Stratum I, since the diggers cut through its debris. But how much later one cannot say; the outlines of the pit were so indistinct near the surface that when you drew the section you had to indicate your uncertainty by using dotted lines to create a stratigraphic impossibility, namely, section lines that cross. Thus you have warned the researcher not to place great weight on any object found in Pit 2021; all one can say is that the pit was dug later than Stratum I. Since the pit could have been refilled with material from any period of the mound's history, there is no way to date any object in it to the Iron Age or to any other period.

Robber Trench 2052, the locus of the second object under study, has similar problems, though not quite so severe. It was clearly dug after Fill 2053 was in place and before the surfaces of Stratum I were laid, most likely in order to rob stone from Wall 2055 of Stratum II (Fig. 3*B*). Like Pit 2021, it was refilled with debris that could have come from any earlier period of the mound. But unlike Pit 2021, Robber Trench 2052 is *sealed* by the surfaces of Stratum I (Fig. 3*A*). Therefore, the researcher knows that any object in Robber Trench 2052 cannot be later than the date of the founding of Stratum I. This provides a *terminus ad quem* or *terminus ante quem* (the expressions are equivalent; see Glossary) for the importation of the object onto the site. In other words, although the fill of Trench 2052 has no upper or higher limit in time (*terminus a quo* or *terminus post quem*) it cannot be later than the origin of Stratum I. The building of Stratum I is the latest possible date that object could have arrived at this site; and since we saw above (p. 29) that Stratum I was built shortly after the destruction of Stratum II, the *terminus ante quem* for the object is the late eighth or, at latest, early seventh century B.C. This may be important information for the researcher, who perhaps was uncertain whether the type of object in question was found in Judah this early.

One would suppose that the researcher would be most confident about the date of the object found on Surface 2058 of Stratum II, but its position on the surface does not by itself date the object to the eighth century. For one thing, some objects can be heirlooms, passed down from previous generations. This is a judgment the researcher will have to make on typological grounds (more later). The stratigraphic question that will give the researcher pause about the object found on Surface 2058 is exactly where on the surface it was discovered. By glancing at the section that you drew (Fig. 3*A*), he or she can see that you found a stratigraphic distinction between Locus 2060, destruction debris from the end of Stratum II, and Locus 2053, fill thrown in before Stratum I was built. If the object was found under Locus 2060, then the chances are excellent that the object was used in Stratum II and thus can exemplify foreign influence in Judah during that period. If, however, it was found in a part of Room A where Fill 2053 rested directly on Surface 2058, then the object might possibly have been thrown in with the fill, a situation similar to that of Robber Trench 2052. If you have published the evidence from your excavation properly, you will have provided the information somewhere to tell the researcher whether to interpret the object as sealed between Debris 2060 and Surface 2058 or between Fill 2053 and the surface.

As for the objects from Loci 2061 and 2048, the researcher will need even more detailed information about the nature of the debris in these loci, information which will in part depend upon your prior judgment during the excavation. We have described Locus 2061 as a layer, banked into the angle formed by the corner of Walls 2055 and 2057 in Stratum II. Since this locus did not extend into the north balk, there is no section drawing to show its stratigraphical position; but you have provided our putative researcher with a verbal description somewhere in the text of the report which indicates that Locus 2061 was sandwiched between Loci 2053 and 2060. For our researcher, however, this is not enough: was Locus 2061, like Locus 2060, part of the destruction debris of Stratum II and thus firmly dated to the eighth century? Or was it more like Locus 2053, a fill, with only an *ante quem* date? How certain can one be that the object from Locus 2061 was part of the culture of the inhabitants of the tell in the eighth century B.C.? Here the researcher must be judicious. If your description of Locus 2061 is offhand or missing entirely, the researcher would be well advised to err on the side of caution and to avoid making the object in question a central piece of evidence. If, however, your report shows that while you were still in the field and able to examine the evidence firsthand, you came to a considered judgment—for example, that Locus 2061 did indeed represent destruction debris—then the researcher may well decide to accept your judgment and to put more weight on that particular object in constructing a synthetic hypothesis.

The researcher will have to ask similar questions about the object found in Locus 2048. Apart from possible contamination from Pit 2035, the debris of this locus appears homogeneous and undisturbed, probably representing the collapsed walls of the stratum. If the object in question was found in the lower levels of this layer, near or on the flagstones of Surface 2051, then chances are good that the object was in use when the stratum was destroyed at the beginning of the sixth century. But again one must exercise caution and judgment. For example, was the object found intact or only as a small fragment? If the latter, it might have been mixed into the mudbricks of the house walls when they were being made at the *beginning* of the stratum, making the *ad quem* date the eighth century instead of the sixth. Or, again, was the object found in the upper levels of the locus, high above the floor level? Such a find spot does not automatically mean that the object cannot be attributed to Stratum I; perhaps the object was sitting on a shelf or in a niche on the inside of the house wall which, when it was destroyed, fell *outward*, leaving the object embedded in the upper side of the wall debris, relatively high above the surface. Again the researcher will look through your report for hints or preferably solid evidence on which to base a decision. But archaeology is an art, not a science; and in the end, critical judgment based on broad knowledge and experience is indispensable.

By now the reader may have long forgotten what precisely we are about, namely deriving common-sense principles to guide us in maximizing the percentage of accurate information recovered in excavating a mound. In fact, despite our proleptic examination of elements of the recording system and even of use of the final publication, we have left you standing atop the mound, poised with pick in hand, yet to open your first square. The principles we have been discussing thus far, an adequate concept of the "pieces" of the mound, what we have here called loci, and a complete and proven recording system are both preliminaries to the actual excavation. But at long last we are ready to dig; and we come to the third common-sense principle, namely control.

The Principle of Control

Early excavators often employed hundreds of workers to cut huge trenches across a mound, stopping only when significant architectural levels were detected. But our faithful guide, common sense, together with an accurate knowledge of the intricacies of stratification leads us to conclude that such digging methods are illegitimate; they are "out of control," destroying more evidence than they recover.

The basic principle we are here calling control can be simply stated: the excavator must be able at each moment during the excavation to distinguish between loci and to remove them in stratigraphic sequence with minimal mixing and confusion. Control depends to a large extent on good digging technique, a detailed description of which would not be appropriate here.[7] But whether a site has been dug with adequate control is of immediate concern to all who want to use the published results, and there are tests that can produce a reasonably accurate estimation. For example, since excavation obviously starts from the top and works down, the excavator is always standing in loosened soil that obscures what lies beneath, making difficult the identification of loci as they emerge. The common-sense solution is to minimize the problem by keeping the loose dirt cleaned up, digging only a small depth at a time, and removing all loose debris before digging deeper. One can judge the care of the excavator on this score by looking at the photographs. Is the digging "clean"? If there are heaps of loose debris

---

7. In addition to the relevant chapters in *A Manual of Field Excavation* cited above, n. 3, see also Kathleen M. Kenyon, *Beginning in Archaeology*, (London: Phoenix House, 1952) and Mortimer Wheeler, *Archaeology from the Earth* (Oxford: Oxford University Press, 1954).

everywhere, it is a "dirty" dig, and valuable evidence is being obscured.

Another gauge of proper control is the adequacy of supervision. To turn gangs of workers loose on a site with only a few supervisors is to guarantee mass destruction of evidence. Small crews under the guidance of untrained, inexperienced, or disorganized supervisors can do nearly as much damage. The adequacy of supervisory control is more difficult to judge from published reports; the size of the staff may look satisfactory, but apart from personal acquaintance there is little basis on which to judge its competence. However, in archaeology as in most enterprises, standards are set and enforced by the person in charge; therefore, the reputation of the skill of the chief excavator will be some gauge of the competency of the staff.

Certainly another test of control is the full use of the tools of proper recording described above. A publication that simply states the conclusions of the excavator without presenting detailed evidence raises the question whether the conclusions are in fact based on solid data or simply on overall impressions. Any publication that does not include measured sections or give evidence of a clear and coherent recording system must raise doubts about whether the digging was under complete control.

A fourth test, which, however, can be made only by experts, is the examination of the pottery attributed to a single stratum to see if it is homogeneous or mixed. Suppose, for example, that a group of loci are presented as the best examples of clearly stratified materials for a particular horizon, but scattered among the pottery published from those loci is a mixture of forms from other periods. If the pattern of mixture is random, then serious questions must be raised about the control of the digging—whether layers were clearly separated, whether pits and fills were properly identified. In fact, the constant inspection of pottery is an indispensable control in the actual excavation process. The buckets of pottery recovered from each locus must be washed and examined closely while the locus is still being dug; for sometimes, despite all the excavator's skill, loci will be mixed together inadvertently, especially in the case of those bothersome pits. When this occurs, the mixture of pottery will turn up in the daily pottery-reading sessions; and before further damage is done, the excavator can return to the field to evaluate the situation and to search for the source of contamination.

If all goes well and if the excavation of the tell is properly done, the result is a clear picture of the architecture and installations of each stratum, plus a series of groups of materials of all sorts, arranged locus by locus in a relative chronological sequence. On occasion, unfortunately rare in Palestinian mounds, something in one or more of these locus groups will provide a peg in absolute chronology on which to hang the relative sequence. For example, in an early excavation at Gezer, the British archaeologist R. A. S. Macalister found two Assyrian tablets that could be dated exactly to 651 and 649 B.C. More often, however, absolute dates can be established only within variable limits through the second of the two basic principles of archaeology, namely typology.

TYPOLOGY

Human culture, like nature itself, astonishes with both its variety and its order. Were we to collect, for example, all the utensils used just to drink liquids, the variety of shapes and materials would at first seem endless. One would quickly notice, however, that despite all the combinations that are possible, the objects would sort themselves into categories that share similar characteristics. For example, in Western countries, one drinks certain liquids most frequently from certain forms —water from a glass, coffee from a cup or mug, wine from a glass with a stem. The glass, true to its name, is almost always composed of that material or of plastic, but almost never of earthenware or porcelain. Cups are made of ceramics, paper, plastic, or metal but rarely glass. Mugs, although a kind of cup, frequently are made of glass, but then they are used almost exclusively to drink cold liquids. Cups and mugs have handles; but one would consider a wine glass with a handle to be "funny," literally and figuratively. In short, we carry with us unconscious but strong cultural assumptions about what different kinds of objects ought to look like and what they ought to be used for, mental templates that allow us to take in and process data. Each of these sets of unconscious assumptions is a *type* which may be made concrete within a broad circle of materials and details but which cannot stray too far without becoming a source of curiosity or confusion. An American visitor to Israel or the Arab countries at first considers it "odd" to see hot tea served in a glass or a cup made of glass. People from England who try to mail a letter in America are surprised to find that one must first open the mailbox before depositing the letter; English pillar boxes simply have open slits to receive the mail. In America and England, one opens a door by turning a knob; east of the English Channel one enters instead by turning a handle. Each variation is a type, which is taken for granted by those in whose culture it is typical and considered different by those with a different mental image.

Even in the most static of human societies, types are constantly changing. To the casual observer all ancient Egyptian art appears the

37

same, but even a neophyte quickly learns to distinguish between a tomb painting of the Old Kingdom and one of the Amarna period. In our own much more fluid culture, it is the constant but unconscious change of types that makes us one day realize that Bermuda shorts or mini skirts are "old fashioned." Typological change can occur by modification within a type, by replacement of one type by something quite different, by abandonment of an old type, or by creation of a new one. Though Bermuda shorts were succeeded by shorter shorts and mini skirts by longer styles, we still recognize in the new fashions the types "shorts" and "skirts." But when a slide rule is replaced by an electronic calculator, we see one type quickly reduced in frequency and its place taken by something new. The demise of the slide rule was occasioned by the arrival of a superior replacement. Other types simply fade away through disuse or disinterest. Still others spring up with no antecedents, such as the phonograph or the airplane.

Typological change proceeds irregularly; it can be rapid in some periods and slow in others. Wars, for obvious reasons, can produce periods of rapid and unexpected change. Who could have predicted in 1905 that the hemline of women's dresses, which had reached the ankle for millennia, would climb to the knees within twenty years? Obviously, World War I with its upheavals had much to do with this and other changes. Geography also affects the rate of change. Cities, the centers of exchange and innovation, evolve more rapidly than outlying districts. Arab women who live in Jerusalem tend to dress in Western fashions; but in the villages, the traditional long embroidered dress is the rule. The phrase "cultural lag," although it has evaluative overtones, is often used to describe the observable variation of the spread of typological change in time or space.

Like biological mutation, typological change does not result in infinite variety. Instead, certain variations become dominant and the rest disappear. One or at most a few new styles or types will prevail. A striking example of this occurred in the countercultures of the 1960s, one of whose mottoes was "Do your own thing." One would have supposed that such exuberant individualism would result in typological anarchy; but on the contrary, the vast majority who adopted this motto chose to "do their own thing" in a remarkably homogeneous style: long hair, headbands, beads, fringed leather jackets, dashikis—in short, not unlimited variety but a clearly recognizable new type.

One learns the characteristics of a type by observation or experience of a number of examples. If a team of extraterrestrial visitors wished to analyze the material culture of an American city, they might begin by constructing typologies of the different buildings. They would visit a sufficient sample of them until patterns began to emerge. They would observe that some buildings were used primarily for places of residence for people and that, although no two were exactly alike, they shared certain common characteristics, such as facilities for storing, preparing, and eating food, for sleeping, for bathing and personal care, for entertaining and relaxation, and so on. Other buildings would be observed to be used for storing goods which people would come to buy. Still other buildings, similar to one another in appearance, would specialize in selling fuel for automobiles. These extraterrestrial visitors would even observe buildings that were empty most of the time but where some earthlings gathered on occasion for strange solemn rituals, which our visitors would probably guess had some cultic significance.

Were the space travelers to concentrate on one specific type of building, they would find it composed of identifiable subtypes, such as residential buildings that contain only one set of basic living facilities, those that contain two complete sets, those that contain three, four, or even hundreds. In studying single-unit dwellings, they might again detect patterns—some built all on one floor, others with two or more stories, some with a small building attached as a shelter for an automobile, others with none.

It is important to note that the creation of types is partly objective and partly subjective. The typologist consciously or unconsciously selects certain features as the most-important ones in defining the type, treating others as secondary or unimportant. The making of types will depend to a large extent on what questions are asked and where the lines are drawn among the variables. Once the essential characteristics and the possible variations of a type have been established, one can identify any specific example as a member of that type. If the identification is correct, then certain conclusions which apply to the type as a whole will also be true of the individual example, such as its date. Indeed, it is as a method of dating that archaeologists have made their greatest use of typology.

In dealing with ancient remains, the archaeologist is analogous to visitors from outer space. Lacking any knowledge of prior finds from the mounds of Palestine, the archaeologist would have to deduce a picture of the culture of each stratum from the artifacts found in that stratum. The first task would be to make typological sense of the recovered material, looking for significant patterns that reveal the mental images or templates that were guiding the makers of the artifacts. Which of the architectural plans bear common characteristics? Of the total number of small objects, how many represent different examples of the same basic type? The relative abundance of pottery, far and away the most common artifact of ancient Palestine, permits fine typological distinctions whereas other objects, more rare, will be represented by so few examples that it will be difficult to be sure of the essential features of the type.

Once the remains of a stratum have been grouped typologically, the archaeologist then compares the types of that stratum with the corresponding types of earlier (deeper) and later (higher) strata to detect the patterns of the inevitable change. Some new types will have been introduced in the interval between strata; others may have vanished entirely. Some continuing types may have changed significantly, others perhaps not at all: stone-grinding vessels from many periods in Palestine are nearly indistinguishable. By comparing a particular type from several successive strata, one can describe the changes that are occurring—the household lamps are developing or losing a rim; the water jars have ceased to have flat bottoms and now are pointed; the bowls have rims that are thicker and more pronounced, or whatever. Archaeologists can only describe the changes that have occurred; they cannot predict what later or earlier forms will look like. Changes that were happening rapidly in a certain direction may slow, stop, go off in another direction, or even reverse themselves. Only one observable pattern seems to interrupt this randomness: namely, that when new types are introduced, the earliest examples tend to have the best form, with later ones becoming more carelessly made, less graceful, and more "debased." Improvements seem to occur most often by the introduction of new types rather than by the gradual evolution of earlier ones.

Although no one can predict the continuing direction of changes in types, a skilled typologist can often predict what forms must have existed between two known types. We can illustrate this in Fig. 4. The changes that occur from Example A to Example B do not permit one

$$? \longrightarrow A \longrightarrow (X) \longrightarrow B \longrightarrow ?$$

Fig. 4. Typological Prediction

to predict what later or earlier examples will look like, but they can give some idea of what to look for as an intermediate stage, Example X, between A and B. If Example A is a jar with no handles and Example B is the same type of jar and stratigraphically later but with vestigial handles, one can expect to find an intermediate form, Example X, which will occur stratigraphically between Examples A and B and which will have serviceable handles, that is, handles added to Type A as a change but which have then become vestigial in Type B.

Typology and Chronology

By combining stratigraphy and typology the archaeologist can construct a relative chronological sequence of a number of different sites. Suppose in excavating Tell 1 (Fig. 5, Col. I), we find four strata, I through IV. Although we may not know the absolute date of any single stratum, it is obvious that the material in Stratum III will be later than that in Stratum IV; how much later will have to be determined on other grounds. Stratum II is later than both Strata III and

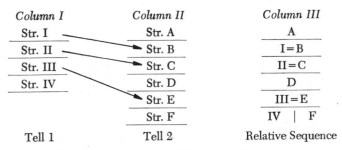

Column I	Column II	Column III
Str. I	Str. A	A
Str. II	Str. B	I = B
Str. III	Str. C	II = C
Str. IV	Str. D	D
	Str. E	III = E
	Str. F	IV | F
Tell 1	Tell 2	Relative Sequence

Fig. 5. Constructing A Relative Sequence

IV, and so on. By studying the materials of each stratum we can attempt to construct typologies for all the different kinds of remains. The typologies of a stratum taken together constitute an *assemblage.* If the assemblage is based on a sufficient sample, it gives us a picture of the culture of the tell at each level. Now we move to a second mound, Tell 2 (Col. II), where we find seven distinct strata, A through F. When we compare the assemblages of each stratum, we find that the culture represented by a stratum in one tell looks very similar to the culture represented in a stratum in the other. The logical conclusion is that the two strata were contemporary, say Strata I and B. Furthermore, Strata II and C correspond, as do III and E. But Tell 1 contains one stratum, IV, for which there is no corresponding horizon in Tell 2. Also, there are three strata, A, D, and F, in Tell 2 that are different from anything in Tell 1. Nevertheless, we can construct the relative sequence shown in Col. III. Only Strata IV and F pose problems. Both are clearly prior to Stratum III = E, but they are not alike and so cannot be contemporary unless they represent cultures that are completely unrelated. Whether one can make any further judgment about the relative chronology of these two strata will depend on a

41

number of factors. If Strata IV and F are clearly in the same cultural tradition as the succeeding strata, one may perhaps guess at the relationship between IV and F on typological grounds. But if either or both Strata IV and F are much different from Strata III and E, then there is no way to correlate them chronologically.

Through examination of more strata in more sites, the relative sequence expands and in theory eventually grows to a coherent series of assemblages, each typologically later than the one preceding. In practice, however, this may take a very long time. In Palestine where stratigraphic archaeology is nearly a hundred years old, the sequence has not yet been fully achieved. Even with pottery and palaeography, the two typological sequences that have received the most attention, there are wide gaps both in our data and among scholars about the interpretation of that data. Most other typologies are only at the rudimentary stage; but as more materials become available from clear stratigraphic contexts, a complete sequence of all artifacts is theoretically possible.

After a series of strata has been compiled, each one representing one static moment in the evolution of the many types represented by ancient Palestinian culture, the next step is to tie the relative sequence to absolute dates. For these the Palestinian archaeologist must turn to Mesopotamia and Egypt where absolute dates can often be calculated astronomically. One obvious way to make correlations is through objects of known date imported into Palestine or, more rarely, through exported Palestinian objects found, for example, in Egyptian tombs. As always, there is room for ambiguity since such objects may give the strata in question only *ante quem* dates. But by sufficient cross correlation, a generally reliable chronological framework for the periods of Palestinian archaeology has slowly been worked out and is constantly being refined (see Appendix).

There are other methods available to the archaeologist to determine the age of a stratum, such as carbon dating, but none of these has as yet achieved the precision produced by typological correlation of human artifacts.

Once the date of a particular stratum or entire horizon has been established along with the types found in it, that information can be used to date those contexts in other sites where examples of the same types are found. Stratigraphy and typology are thus interdependent. On the one hand the stratified groups of materials provide the data for the abstraction of types and their patterns of change and distribution. On the other hand, once the types are dated, they fix the chronology of other stratigraphic contexts in which the same type is found. New stratigraphy may also provide information to refine the types further and to make more precise the date.

Ceramic Typology

As far as Palestine is concerned, pottery is far and away the most useful of the typologies. After its first appearance in the area some time before 5000 B.C., it is found virtually at all inhabited sites. Pottery is fragile and easily broken; only the rare sample survives long after its time of manufacture to become an heirloom. Once broken, it is usually discarded, although instances of ancient repair are known. Given pottery's fragility and frequent replacement, forms found smashed in destruction debris will almost certainly represent pottery made a few years before the end of the stratum. Another advantage of this rapid turnover is the relatively swift change in typological development; the potter did not have models from hundreds of years earlier to serve as patterns. There were only the potter's own mental image of a certain shape plus existing examples no more than thirty to forty years old, combined with the potter's empirical sensitivity to what would "work." The result was not wild innovation in what was, after all, a conservative craft, but a more rapid change than in objects or features that endured and were rarely replaced. Finally, pottery has the typological advantage of ubiquity. Pottery was used in every home from rich to poor. The average tell yields sherds, restorable vessels, and even the occasional unbroken pot in such quantities that one is hard pressed to maintain proper control of the flow.

The typological advantages of pottery have firmly established it as the principal source of chronology for the historic and late prehistoric periods in Palestine.[8] All who study Palestinian archaeology must develop a minimal knowledge of the forms and characteristics of each period, though few have the fine eye and memory for form and detail to become truly expert. There is a vast body of lore on the subject, and no more than some general principles can be offered here.

When experts in the ceramic history of Palestine examine a specimen to determine to what type it belongs, and thus its chronological range, they have basically five criteria in mind: (1) form, (2) form variant, (3) decoration, (4) ware, and (5) technique of manufacture.

Form. From the foregoing discussion of typology, one would cor-

8. The standard work is by Ruth Amiran et al, *Ancient Pottery of the Holy Land* (New Brunswick, N.J.: Rutgers University Press, 1970).

rectly assume that the pottery forms found in Palestine over the millennia are not infinitely varied. Form follows function, and the successive cultures of ancient Palestine were all basically agrarian. Large jars were needed for storage of grain, wine, and oil; juglets for dipping small quantities of liquids from larger jars; pots for cooking; bowls and plates for eating; jars, pitchers, and cups for fetching, pouring, and drinking water and wine; vessels for use as lamps. Indeed, most of the names we use for the basic repertoire of forms describe the known or presumed function—pitcher, cooking pot, storage jar (*pithos*), lamp—rather than the vessel's shape. Some forms, such as lamps or storage jars, appear in stratum after stratum for many hundreds of years. Others occur in Palestine only in one or two periods, especially imported forms such as the one-handled Cypriote "milk-bowl" which is confined to the Late Bronze Age.[9]

Form variant. Two jars from Palestine, both classified as storage jars, may have nothing in common beyond the name we give them and their similar size. Obviously they come from different cultural periods. Their differences may be due to distant separation in time, although demonstrably connected by many intermediate forms, or the differences may be due to the death of one ceramic tradition and the introduction of a totally different one. A good example of gradual change over time is the cooking pot which can be traced step by step in its evolving form for well over one thousand years (Fig. 6). As an example of a complete shift, we may cite one dramatic change at the end of the Middle Bronze I period when the flat-bottomed storage jar became extinct. Thereafter, all storage jars without exception had pointed or rounded bases.

Cooking Pot	1800 B.C.		1550 B.C.		1200 B.C.	1000 B.C.	600 B.C.
Rim Development		Middle Bronze II		Late Bronze		Iron I	Iron II

FIG. 6. DEVELOPMENT OF THE COOKING POT
(*Used by permission of J. D. Seger*)

9. Ibid., pp. 172–73.

The neophyte quickly learns the nature and dates of the obvious changes such as the one just cited. Only the expert eye, however, can evaluate those forms which are undergoing slow and often subtle change. Changes occur most obviously in the details—whether the rims are thick or thin, elaborate or plain; whether the bases are shaped like a ring or are flat like a disk; whether the handles are flat, oval, or triangular in section; whether the handles are attached horizontally or vertically—and in dozens of other variations of the parts of the vessel, individually and in relation to each other. Again the beginner learns to recognize some features immediately, such as the elaborate ledge-handles of the Early Bronze Age, the thick heavy bases of late Judean lamps, or the elegant footed bowls and chalices of the Middle Bronze period. However, to learn the more subtle variations requires the patient study and tracing of dozens of drawings of well-stratified examples and, more especially, the physical handling of hundreds of pots, both whole forms and sherds.

Decoration. Surface decoration plays a much less important role in typological analysis of Palestinian pottery than form simply because in most periods decoration is simple or lacking altogether. The most common form of surface decoration was burnishing, that is, polishing the plain clay surface to seal the pores and to create a lustrous finish. In the Middle Bronze IIA period, for example, the burnishing was so smooth and brilliant that no individual marks of the burnish tool are visible, while the later Iron II period is typified by plates with no burnishing on the exterior surface but with ring burnishing on the inside. (Ring burnishing is an effect created by placing the burnishing tool in the center of the form and then as the wheel turns rapidly, moving it to the outer edge, creating a tight spiral pattern of alternate burnished and unburnished "rings.") Painted designs occur especially in the Late Bronze and Early Iron ages. Other kinds of decoration found in various periods are combing, wiping, incising, stippling, the application of moldings, and others.

Ware. Ware refers to the appearance of the fired clay of which the vessel is made, both on the surface and in section. Of concern here are the color, the purity of the clay, its hardness, the type of inclusions, even the sound it makes when sherds are struck together or poured out on the examining table. Potters of some periods were more skillful in preparing clay than those of others. This skill did not necessarily improve over time; the ware of the Middle Bronze II period is far superior to that of the Early Iron Age some 500 years later. Again, although some features of ware are quickly learned, such as the shiny silica inclusions mixed with the clay of cooking pots to permit heating without breakage, the study of ware is still in its infancy; ware is only now beginning to undergo close scrutiny.[10]

Manufacture. In early periods, pottery was all handmade, built up in segments or by coils of clay. Although some pottery continued to be handmade, the fast wheel, which permitted the throwing of elaborate shapes, came into general use in the second millennium B.C. The large jars of the Middle Bronze I period from the beginning of that millennium provide an interesting example of transition: the bodies of the jars are handmade, but the rims are wheelmade and fastened onto the finished body, leaving a telltale seam which is easily felt inside the neck. Skill and technique of firing also vary from period to period: high temperatures in an oxydizing atmosphere burn out the organic elements in the clay, producing the typical reds, buffs, and creams of most Palestinian pottery. In some periods a reducing atmosphere was produced in the kiln, which resulted in a black finish, such as the distinctive black dipper juglets of the Iron II period. Recently, it has been proposed that a close analysis of the way in which pottery was made can serve as an alternative to the traditional emphasis on variation of form as a way of dating pottery. Regardless of the ultimate fate of this particular hypothesis, such study will yield valuable information about how the relationship between the potter and the clay affects typological change.[11]

---

10. See Albert E. Glock, "Homo Faber: The Pot and the Potter at Taanach," *BASOR* 219 (1975):9–28.

11. H. J. Franken, *Excavations at Tell Deir ʿAllā I,* Part Two; idem, *In Search of the Jericho Potters* (Amsterdam and Oxford: North Holland Publishing Co., 1974). For an excellent statement of the classic methodology in the use of pottery for dating, see John S. Holladay, Jr., "Of Sherds and Strata: Contributions toward an Understanding of the Archaeology of the Divided Monarchy," *Magnalia Dei: The Mighty Acts of God,* ed. F. M. Cross, Werner E. Lemke, and P. D. Miller, Jr. (Garden City, N.Y.: Doubleday, 1976), pp. 254–59.

III
Archaeological Publications and Their Use

Over the past seventy-five to one hundred years, a considerable body of excavated material has accumulated from Palestine, much of it from periods contemporaneous with the events recorded in the Old Testament. The critical student of the Old Testament comes to this material with the hope that it will answer some specific questions about the biblical text and the world from which it sprang. What did Jerusalem look like in the days of Isaiah or Jeremiah or Nehemiah? What do we know about Canaanite high places? When the Philistines charged the Israelites a pim or a third of a shekel of silver to sharpen certain tools (1 Sam. 13:21), how expensive was this? Or more general questions can be asked: What does archaeology say about the historical memory of the Bible? Can the stories of the patriarchs be connected with known historical events or a specific cultural background? The biblical student justifiably expects that the mounting archaeological evidence should speak to these and similar questions.

Those with questions about the historical and cultural context in which the Old Testament was born have a variety of aids to which they can turn for answers. The most common of these are the semi-popular volumes that bear a variant of the title *The Bible and Archaeology* or *The Archaeology of Palestine,* a representative list of which appears at the end of Chapter I. Although these works differ in format, approach, or presupposition, they predictably cover many of the same major sites, monuments, objects, inscriptions, and interpretive theories. Despite this duplication, such volumes will continue to be written and purchased at a steady pace, because discovery never ceases. With the details of the total picture in constant flux, this year's summary is quickly outdated. These volumes are intended for the intelligent layperson and require no previous background. There are

47

also two major journals in English which can help the general reader keep up to date: the semipopular but authoritative *Biblical Archeologist*, published by the American Schools of Oriental Research, and the more popular *Biblical Archaeology Review*.

In contrast to the quantity of useful volumes of popular or semipopular synthesis, there is a distressing lack of such works at the technical level. It is surprising, for example, that no volume exists which brings together in a complete and critical way the sum of information about Palestine in the Bronze Age or the Iron Age—city plans; house plans; synchronic tables of occupation; objects of cult, agriculture, and daily life; the epigraphic evidence; and so on. Nor has much technical synthesis been done at that point where it would be most useful to biblical scholars and students, namely in the biblical commentaries. By and large, biblical commentators are trained only in literary techniques, which they often handle with great critical skill and independence of judgment. But when a problem arises in the text which calls for archaeological comment, they not infrequently refer the reader to secondary sources with no explanation of the issues and with no independent critical discussion. Most commentators do not even make use of archaeology where it can contribute best, namely in illustrating the material culture of a given period, either in general or in terms of a specific reference in the text.[1] Because of the concrete nature of archaeological evidence, it is best communicated visually, in photographs, drawings, and plans. And yet as one leafs through the pages of current critical works, even those on books such as Kings that cry out for archaeological commentary, one finds only the rare map or diagram, and sometimes nothing at all.[2]

Given the lack of up-to-date critical synthesis, either at the technical level or in the commentaries, the biblical student who wishes to pursue in depth a problem in Palestinian archaeology will have to do so in the primary literature. The critical use of this material is not simple, and the researcher needs to keep several things in mind.

In the first place, one must of necessity use archaeological publications, which vary enormously in quality and reliability. In biblical criticism one may usually pass over the works of scholars who employ

1. To be helpful, such works need not be commentaries in the traditional sense; Othmar Keel presents an original approach in several of his works, e.g., *The Symbolism of the Biblical World* (London: SPCK, 1978), in which he has collected hundreds of illustrations that illuminate the Psalms.
2. For an exception and an excellent example of how archaeology can contribute to biblical commentary, see Edward F. Campbell, Jr., *Ruth, The Anchor Bible* (Garden City, N.Y.: Doubleday, 1975).

poor or outdated methods to concentrate on more recent figures and a few giants of the past. Not so in archaeology. As we noted in the preceding chapter, the excavation of any particular piece of archaeological data can occur only once. There is no way to repeat the experiment, as it were, even if it was done incompetently. Take, for example, the site of Tell Zakarīyeh, generally identified as biblical Azekah. Our sole source of information about this site is the report of an excavation conducted in 1898–99 when archaeological method was still primitive. We have no choice but to use the materials as published, with all the inevitable problems.[3] In short, the archaeological researcher willy-nilly must often use material that was recovered by all sorts of methods and published by a wide range of individuals who vary greatly in skill and insight. Obviously, therefore, the researcher must develop a fine critical sense about archaeological reports, being able to decide how far to trust the conclusions of the excavators and whether any specific material can be used for detailed study or only to fill out the details of a picture drawn from better evidence, and so on.

Without doubt, the most fruitful step toward learning to read archaeological reports critically is acquiring some actual experience in the field. By observing and participating in a dig, one gains a number of valuable bases for judgment—a concrete image of what stratigraphy is, an appreciation of the practical difficulties of stratigraphic excavation, a sense of the inevitable limitations and ambiguities of excavated evidence, an opportunity to hear, use, and learn archaeological vocabulary, to see and handle archaeological materials, and to acquire a reservoir of visual images to give actuality to the words and drawings of an archaeological report. Beginning in the 1960s many digs began to use volunteer laborers, and such experience is now not hard to come by. Anyone who intends to make extensive use of archaeological publications in biblical research should give high priority to spending a summer or more in actual excavation.

Even without field experience, however, there is much one can do to break through the intimidating façade of an elegant folio report volume. First of all, one must realize that one need not be an expert in archaeology in order to find answers to certain kinds of questions. Certainly if one wished to compile a list of excavated Israelite cities possibly destroyed by the Assyrians in their campaigns in the 730s and 720s B.C., one would need the requisite expertise in ceramic typology of the

---

3. F. J. Bliss and R. A. S. Macalister, *Excavations in Palestine during the Years 1898–1900* (London: Committee of the Palestine Exploration Fund, 1902).

Iron II period to test the dates given to the strata in question by the excavators, which is a fairly sophisticated exercise. But if one wished simply to map the geographical distribution of Assyrian "palace ware," a style of pottery imported by the Assyrians into Palestine, one would need to know only that examples had been recovered from a site; one would not have to make a critical judgment about larger issues of excavation method, analysis of evidence, or quality of publication.

If the person researching archaeological reports does not have the technical knowledge, primarily ceramic and stratigraphic, on which to base an independent judgment of published results, there are nevertheless clear signals by which to judge the quality of a report. As one would suspect, the period in which an excavation was carried out can provide some clues to its reliability. For example, it was not until the Germans dug at Jericho in 1908–09 that any Palestinian excavation had an adequate staff or properly recorded the architecture. The all-important ceramic chronology of the country was not firmly settled until W. F. Albright published a series of reports between 1932 and 1943 on the results of his work at Tell Beit Mirsim; and not until Kathleen Kenyon's work at Jericho in the 1950s did the proper analysis of debris layers and their recording in measured sections have a wide impact on excavation technique. But progress is neither steady nor consistent, and some excavations of even the 1960s and 1970s were open to valid criticism for inadequate staffing, recording, and stratigraphic methodology. Moreover, there are honest philosophical differences among excavators on points of method. Some feel, for example, that the presence of balks in an area under excavation can do as much harm as good by impeding the recovery of restorable pottery vessels, pieces of which are concealed in the balk, and by carving up the architecture into artificial segments, preventing the recovery of overall plans.[4] Thus, the date of a report alone is insufficient to release a researcher from the need of forming an independent judgment.

Many of the questions that one must learn to ask of an archaeological publication have already been demonstrated by example in Chapter II in the section on stratigraphy and can be summarized quickly here: Is the excavator self-conscious about excavation method, or does the report reflect unexamined assumptions? Is the dig staff sufficiently large? Does it include the necessary technicians, draftsmen,

---

4. Yohanan Aharoni, "Remarks on the 'Israeli' Method of Excavation," *EI* 11 (1973): 48–53 (English summary, 23°). Aharoni, however, concedes the need to use balks; the unresolved matter is how to maximize recovery of information, given this necessity. For an attempt at a mediating position, see William G. Dever, "Two Approaches to Archaeological Method—The Architectural and the Stratigraphic," *EI* 11 (1973):1°–8°.

photographers, and enough field personnel to give close oversight to field operations? (The words "enough" and "sufficient" are obviously relative; a very small operation may be staffed adequately by three or four people if they have among them the requisite skills.) Does the excavator's concept of "locus" or whatever corresponding term is used, permit a sufficiently detailed analysis of the "pieces" of the mound, or is the concept so broad that mixing of materials is inevitable? Judging from the written report, was the excavator alert to pits, fills, and other disturbances? Or does he or she tend to treat everything between surfaces as homogeneous? Are architectural plans detailed, or are they impressionistic and schematic? Do they provide sufficient levels, or are they simply two-dimensional? Do the photographs reveal care and control in the excavation, or do they, for example, show gangs of unsupervised laborers with heaps of loose debris lying about? Does the report include drawings of sections or show awareness of their necessity? If sections are published, are they schematic or measured? Do they show the connecting debris layers or only the walls? Finally—the crucial test—is it possible, working from the publication alone, to reconstruct the stratigraphic context from which a particular find was recovered? These common-sense tests require no expertise in ceramic typology or in any other technical aspect of Palestinian archaeology and can be applied to modern as well as early digs, to preliminary or to final reports. Not all uncertainties about the reliability of a report will be resolved by these tests. Nor do they help to settle problems of conflicting judgments by scholars of apparently equal qualifications who may disagree about the date of an object or stratum. In the final analysis, one cannot simply categorize any dig report as "good" or "bad"; each must be scrutinized carefully and used with a clear sense of the inherent limits of the evidence and of the exact uses one wishes to make of it.

There is another problem for which the beginning researcher should be prepared, namely that excavators systematize and present their evidence in quite different styles. Systems of numbering squares and loci and of recording and referring to objects and architecture are idiosyncratic to each archaeological publication. Most digs designate strata by letters or numbers from the top down (latest to earliest), but some publications number from the bottom up. The words "locus," "phase," "stratum," and so on are used in different ways; and, not infrequently, the reader is forced to derive the sense of such terms from observation of the excavator's usage. In short, each dig report must be tediously deciphered before one can use it properly; sometimes, as in the case of the publications of Tell en-Naṣbeh, cracking the system is virtually impossible.[5] Usually, however, reading the preface or the section on method, in the case of a final report, and patient application of common sense will turn the trick.

Finally, one confusing disagreement in chronological terminology must be signalized (see Table below). About 1950 B.C. a sharp cultural shift occurred in Palestine, which was marked by a rapid revival of urban life after an apparent hiatus of hundreds of years. However, when the original nomenclature of periods was adopted for the country (Table, Col. I), this shift was still unclear. Consequently, the period of the new culture (Middle Bronze II) was combined with the last phase of the older one (Middle Bronze I), and the whole was called the Middle Bronze Age. Now that the evidence for the shift has emerged, it is apparent that the classical system of names for the cultural phases no longer corresponds with historical reality: what was called the Middle Bronze Age needs to be divided. Numerous suggestions for a new system of nomenclature have emerged, but because none has received the status of consensus, considerable confusion has resulted. One of the most influential variants is that of Kathleen Kenyon (Table, Col. II), who substituted the term Intermediate Early Bronze–Middle Bronze for Middle Bronze I and then renumbered the other periods of the Middle Bronze Age. By comparing across Columns I and II, one can see the problem: when reading Kenyon or one of her followers, one must remember that what she calls MB I is termed MB IIA by many others, and so forth. Most recent writers are agreed that the classical system is now inadequate, but they have preferred

TABLE—VARIATIONS IN NOMENCLATURE FOR THE
MIDDLE BRONZE AGE

Column I Classic Terminology	Column II Kenyon's Terminology
Middle Bronze I	Intermediate Early Bronze– Middle Bronze
CULTURAL SHIFT, ca. 1950 B.C.	
Middle Bronze IIA	Middle Bronze I
Middle Bronze IIB	Middle Bronze IIA
Middle Bronze IIC	Middle Bronze IIB

5. C. C. McCown, *Tell en-Naṣbeh I: Archaeological and Historical Results;* John C. Wampler, *Tell en-Naṣbeh II: The Pottery* (Berkeley and New Haven: The Palestine Institute of the Pacific School of Religion and the American Schools of Oriental Research, 1947).

solutions that do not involve renumbering the other periods of the Middle Bronze Age.[6]

TYPES OF ARCHAEOLOGICAL PUBLICATIONS

Armed with the critical understanding of stratigraphy, typology, and archaeological publication acquired thus far in Chapters II and III, we are ready to enter the thicket of the literature to search for the answers to whatever questions we have in mind. Before plunging in, however, let us stop to regard this thorny terrain to see what different kinds of material it contains. For our purposes, we shall distinguish three major categories: (a) primary reports, (b) criticism, and (c) synthesis.

Primary reports. Excavation projects or new isolated finds are first published in reports, which can be either popular or technical in style. For the most part, these reports fall into three divisions: current reports, preliminary reports, and final reports.

Current reports can be informal and nontechnical, intended for the general public, or brief technical or semitechnical reports for the audience of specialists. The former can range widely in reliability and completeness. The spectrum shades from the reports of journalists in the popular press through more serious accounts such as those in the *Illustrated London News* and on to more specialized magazines and semipopular journals, such as *Biblical Archeologist, Biblical Archaeology Review, Archaeology, National Geographic,* the *Newsletter* of the American Schools of Oriental Research, and others. These reports tend to be well illustrated and written for a popular audience. They usually treat matters of general interest—the recovery of a new Dead Sea scroll after the Arab–Israeli Six Day War in 1967, the finding of horned altars at Dan and Beer-sheba, the results of the new Jerusalem excavations, and so on.

The second type of current report, that written for other specialists, briefly summarizes recent results of ongoing field work or describes individual finds of unusual interest, such as ostraca or other inscriptional material, unusual or important objects, findings which resolve some long-standing problem or challenge common assumptions, and so on. The excavation summaries usually present the results of a single season, sometimes more, with only a few or no illustrations and no attempt to give the evidence upon which the published conclusions are based. Such reports appear routinely in the *Israel Exploration Journal*

6. Another variation in Kenyon's terminology should also be mentioned, namely the term Proto-Urban for certain groups in the complicated transition from the Chalcolithic to the Early Bronze Age. However, this is only an added term, not necessitating a change in the classical terminology of adjacent periods.

(for Israel) and in the section "Chronique archéologique" in the *Revue Biblique* (for Israel and Jordan), although as in the case of the popular report, there is no uniform pattern.[7]

These current reports are of mixed value to researchers. Newspaper stories are frequently distorted or misleading but are sometimes the only information available. Seasonal summaries written by the excavator or other staff member are based on the evidence as currently understood and represent conclusions that may need correction. Thus, the warning to be issued below about citing data from preliminary reports applies all the more to current reports.

Preliminary reports are technical summaries of one or more seasons of excavation describing the important results with some drawings, plans, and photographs.[8] They are thus much more complete than current reports and tend to be addressed more to scholars than to the public. They can be found scattered throughout the journals that specialize in Palestinian archaeology or in separate volumes, monographs, or annuals.[9] Usually, the series of preliminary reports from one site will appear in subsequent years of the same journal or publication, although one dare not take this for granted.

Typically, the preliminary report describes the season or seasons under review from the point of view of the process of excavation. Each field or site of excavation around the mound is dealt with in turn, often without any attempt yet to correlate strata between fields. Since preliminary reports describe work in progress, they are subject to revision by evidence from later seasons. Thus, if a researcher finds a piece of information in an early preliminary report, he or she dare not cite that datum without checking all subsequent current, preliminary, or final reports to make sure that it has withstood the test of later seasons of

7. A complete current record of archaeological activity in Israel appears in *Hadashot Arkeologiot,* published in Hebrew by the Israeli Department of Antiquities.

8. Preliminary reports can usually be identified by their titles which customarily contain the name of the site, the year(s) of the season(s) reported, and frequently the words "preliminary report," e.g., Kevin G. O'Connell, S. J., D. Glenn Rose, and Lawrence E. Toombs, "Tell el-Ḥesī, 1977," *PEQ* 110 (1978):75–90; David Ussishkin, "Excavations at Tel Lachish—1973–1977: Preliminary Report," *Tel Aviv* 5 (1978):1–97.

9. The major technical periodicals and serials in Palestinian archaeology are the *Annual of the American Schools of Oriental Research,* the *Annual of the Department of Antiquities of Jordan,* 'Atiqot (Hebrew and English), *Bulletin of the American Schools of Oriental Research, Bulletin of the Israel Exploration Society* (Hebrew) which continues the *Bulletin of the Jewish Palestine Exploration Society* (Hebrew), *Eretz-Israel* (Hebrew and other European languages, usually English), *Israel Exploration Journal, Journal of the Palestine Oriental Society,*° *Levant, Liber Annuus Studii Biblici Franciscani* (usually Italian), *Palestine Exploration Fund Annual,*° *Palestine Exploration Quarterly* which continues the *Palestine Exploration Fund—Quarterly Statement, Palästina Jahrbuch des Deutschen Evangelischen Instituts für Altertumswissenschaft des Heiligen Landes zu Jerusalem,*° *Qedem, Quarterly of the Department of Antiquities in Palestine,*° *Revue Biblique, Tel Aviv, Zeitschrift des Deutschen Palästina-Vereins.*
°Titles marked by an asterisk are no longer published.

excavation or more detailed study. As we saw in the example of Tower 5017 at Gezer cited in Chapter II, reinterpretation or restratification of evidence is sometimes necessary.

Unfortunately, too many excavation projects never advance beyond the preliminary report. In fact, some digs have published nothing beyond brief current reports. Excavators are only human; and whereas digging is glamorous, exhilarating, rewarding, and social, preparation of the material for publication is tedious, frustrating, wearisome, and lonely. Furthermore, many excavators eager to get their projects into the field, fail to plan ahead for the large expenditures of time and money required for publication. Skilled draftsmen, photographers, and administrative assistants must be hired, space for work and storage rented, scientific tests run, and international travel costs for staff paid. The volumes themselves are expensive to produce and rarely sell enough copies to break even. For all these reasons and more, sometimes including the death of the excavator, the results of many projects —Arad (the citadel), Dothan, Hebron, Tell el-Farah (Tirzah), Tell el-Jerisheh, Tell el-Kheleifeh, and Tell Qasile, to pick only a random cross section of some of the most prominent—are available thus far only in preliminary or current reports. Other projects, such as Jerusalem, Gezer, Masada, and Shechem, have yet to publish fully, which leaves much material unavailable and many questions unanswered. If all goes well, however, eventually a complete presentation of the finds along with the best interpretation of the excavator will appear in the third of the major types of primary reports, the final report.

Final reports vary in nature and purpose, but in general they bring together the data from all seasons of excavation, publishing the finds in detail, correlating strata among the separate areas on the mound, and constructing a coherent picture of the mound's occupational history.[10] Since even those projects that do push through to final publication not infrequently take decades to do so, the excavator will sometimes anticipate the final report by getting out a synthetic but still tentative treatment in a popular vein—hence, such volumes as *Digging up Jericho* and *Digging up Jerusalem* by Kathleen Kenyon, *Hazor: The Rediscovery of a Great Citadel of the Bible* by Yigael Yadin, and *Shechem: The Biography of a Biblical City*, revised edition by G. Ernest Wright and E. F. Campbell, Jr. (forthcoming).

10. Like preliminary reports, final reports often can be recognized by their titles, which frequently comprise the name of the site, a subtitle delimiting the scope of a particular volume, and the number of the volume in the series, if more than one, e.g., *Lachish II: The Fosse Temple; Excavations at Jericho I: The Tombs Excavated in 1952–54; The Early Bronze Age Sanctuary at Ai (et-Tell), No. 1*, etc.

The daunting task of preparing a multivolume final report has spawned a new hybrid publication which J. S. Holladay, Jr., has dubbed the expanded preliminary report.[11] This in effect is a book-length preliminary report in lieu of a final report, presenting more evidence than a preliminary report but less than a final one. Such volumes can be produced more quickly than a final report; and, if there is good reason to believe that the choice is between such reports and none at all, then they certainly have a place. But since they are published by season before the excavators have had the benefit of further investigation or the critique of their ideas by colleagues, using them requires the same caution and checking of later results as in using a preliminary report, placing the burden of synthesis on the researcher. Certainly the pattern of preliminary report by season followed by prompt and full final publication is the ideal, albeit an increasingly difficult one to achieve.[12]

If there is any summary of this discussion of the types of primary excavation reports, it is simply a fair warning that the researcher will have to trace carefully the course of publication, accepting the fact that every dig will follow a different pattern. Some go from current reports to final reports without producing preliminary reports. Some, because of the death or disinterest of the excavator, never go beyond preliminary or even current reports. Current reports certainly and sometimes even preliminary reports appear unpredictably in different publications. Final reports can be published years later by persons who were not even present during the digging. In short, the system of publication is irregular, uncertain, and wasteful of excavated evidence. For some practical hints to thread the maze, see the section below on "Finding the Literature."

Criticism. To speak of raw data in archaeology is misleading. The excavation and analysis of stratigraphy, the definition of types, the selection and organization of data for publication, and the interpretation of the significance of the data are all shaped by the perspicacity, good judgment, and informed intuition of the excavator, just as in any other area of empirical humanistic investigation. Even the best efforts of the most learned and skilled excavators will not be beyond criticism by peers and colleagues. However, as explained above, the primary archaeological data, once published, achieve a kind of immortality.

11. Review of *Beer-sheba I: Excavations at Tell Beer-sheba, 1969–1971 Seasons,* ed. Yohanan Aharoni, *JBL* 96 (1977):281.
12. Other examples of the expanded preliminary report, in addition to *Beer-sheba I* (preceding note), are Aharoni's reports on Ramat Raḥel and the first two Gezer volumes by W. G. Dever and H. D. Lance et al.

Subsequent critics rarely republish the material, they only comment on it; the original publication remains the primary source. Thus, there can grow up in relation to the primary publications a body of critical literature—reviews, studies, and so on—which is often as important as the original publication itself. The publications of the Oriental Institute excavations at Megiddo are magnificent to behold and full of priceless data; but to utilize them properly, one must be aware of the important critiques of W. F. Albright, K. M. Kenyon, G. E. Wright, and others (see Chapter IV). Sometimes the opinion of later critics gains general acceptance and supplants the interpretation of the excavators; sometimes the commentators disagree among themselves as vigorously as with the excavator. Only through familiarity with subsequent commentary can one gain a sense of what data may be used as published, what may be used as reinterpreted, and what must be used with caution. The goal, of course, should be to become sufficiently well acquainted with the issues and the evidence to be able to formulate an independent judgment.

In addition to reading subsequent opinion, one must also be alert to new digging at a site. Again taking Megiddo as an example, one must be aware that in a new dig, Yigael Yadin proved that the famous stables, attributed by the original excavators to Solomon, date to a later period, probably the time of Ahab.[13] Gradually, these new findings work their way into the handbooks and encyclopedias, but the effect of new data can be so revolutionary that to base an argument on such slowly evolving secondary sources is to risk instant obsolescence. In short, interpretation of any particular archaeological datum is a continuing trialogue among the original publication, relevant new finds, and critical commentators. One can never take the word of the excavator as final, no matter how imposing the "final" report volume which contains it.

Synthesis. This third major kind of literature in Palestinian archaeology consists of books and articles that seek to pull together data from many sites to create a coherent synchronic sketch of some period or aspect of ancient Palestinian culture, to trace diachronically the development of a type or site, or to summarize current knowledge of some topic or other. Since technical synthesis is based on library and museum work and lacks the glamour of field excavation, it has suffered from neglect, as noted above. The works that do exist are generally recognizable from their titles, for example, *Ancient Pottery of the Holy*

13. See, for example, Yigael Yadin, "New Light on Solomon's Megiddo," *BA* 23 (1960): 62–68.

Land,[14] "The Beginning of the Middle Bronze Age in Syria–Palestine,"[15] or "The Four-Room House—Its Situation and Function in the Israelite City."[16]

FINDING THE LITERATURE

Now that we have some sense of the major kinds of technical archaeological literature, their purpose, content, and limitations, let us observe how the researcher finds a path through this literary forest.

First let us describe some of the major sources of bibliography that are of especial use for Palestinian archaeology. For the sake of brevity, we shall assume familiarity with the general indexes and bibliographical tools for the humanities in general and religion in particular that are available in most university and seminary libraries. Also, we shall have to confine ourselves to those tools that are the most useful and will in turn lead the researcher not only to specific items but to other bibliographical sources.

Abbreviation   *Item*

BRL[2]   Kurt Galling, ed. *Biblisches Reallexikon,* 2d ed. Handbuch zum Alten Testament, Reihe 1/1. Tübingen: Mohr, 1977.
A technical encyclopedia of information on sites and objects mentioned in the Bible. Illustrated. Abundant bibliography.

EAEHL   Michael Avi-Yonah and Ephraim Stern, eds. *Encyclopedia of Archaeological Excavations in the Holy Land.* 4 vols. Englewood Cliffs, N.J.: Prentice-Hall; and Jerusalem: Israel Exploration Society and Massada Press, 1975–78.
A summary of results of excavations at all major sites in Israel plus many in Jordan as well. Profusely illustrated. Bibliography accompanies each article.

EJ   *Encyclopaedia Judaica.* New York: Macmillan; and Jerusalem: Keter Publishing House, 1971.
Many articles on archaeological and biblical topics. Bibliography accompanies each article.

Elenchus   *Elenchus Bibliographicus Biblicus.*
From 1920 to 1967 a section in the journal *Biblica,* but a separate publication since 1968. The most complete collection of bibliography in Bible and related issues. Includes books, periodical articles, and reviews. Many useful indexes.

14. Ruth Amiran (New Brunswick, N.J.: Rutgers University Press, 1970).
15. William G. Dever, *Magnalia Dei: The Mighty Acts of God,* ed. F. M. Cross, W. E. Lemke, and P. D. Miller, Jr. (Garden City, N.Y.: Doubleday, 1976), pp. 3–38.
16. Y. Shiloh, *IEJ* 20 (1970):180–90.

A brief guide in English to the use of *Elenchus* appears in Vol. 57 (1976), xlvi–xlviii.

IDB George Arthur Buttrick, ed. *The Interpreter's Dictionary of the Bible*. 4 vols. Keith Crim, ed. *Supplementary Volume*. Nashville: Abingdon Press, 1962 and 1976.
Biblical encyclopedia with articles on all sites and objects mentioned in the Bible. Bibliography accompanies each article.

IZBG *Internationale Zeitschriftenschau für Bibelwissenschaft und Grenzgebiete* (1951–).
Abstracts in German of all biblical and relevant archaeological periodicals including annuals and occasional volumes. Broader in range than *OTA*. Published annually.

OTA *Old Testament Abstracts* (1978–).
Abstracts in English of all articles published in Old Testament and relevant archaeological journals, but with a smaller selection of journals on the ancient Near East outside of Palestine than in *IZBG* or *Elenchus*. Also does not include annuals or occasional volumes such as the *Annual of the American Schools of Oriental Research*, *Eretz-Israel*, *Levant*, or others. Published three times a year.

OTBL *Old Testament Book List* (1940, 1946–).
Published annually by the British Society for Old Testament Study. Early lists are collected in the following volumes: H. H. Rowley, ed., *Eleven Years of Bible Bibliography (1946–56)*; G. W. Anderson, ed., *A Decade of Bible Bibliography (1957–66)*; and P. R. Ackroyd, ed., *Bible Bibliography 1967–73*, all published by Basil Blackwell in Oxford. Contains brief reviews of a wide range of recent books on Old Testament and related topics, including a section on "Archaeology and Epigraphy."

Permucite Index W. T. Claassen, ed. *O.T./A.N.E. Permucite Index: An Exhaustive Interdisciplinary Indexing System for Old Testament Studies, Ancient Near Eastern Studies*. Stellenbosch: Infodex, 1978–.
A system of indexing periodical articles in terms of the works cited in their footnotes. Invaluable in following the debate on a specific issue, such as the critical debate on primary archaeological material. Covers broad range of periodicals and occasional volumes.

Thomsen Peter Thomsen, ed. *Die Palästina-Literatur*. 8 vols. The last volume was published in 1972 by Akademie Verlag, Berlin.
Exhaustive topical bibliography of all works on the history and archaeology of Palestine from 1878 into the late 1940s.

Especially valuable for the early years before many of the current bibliographical tools began.

Vogel Eleanor K. Vogel. "Bibliography of Holy Land Sites." *Hebrew Union College Annual* 42 (1971):1–96. Reprinted separately as *Bibliography of Holy Land Sites Compiled in Honor of Dr. Nelson Glueck*. Cincinnati: Hebrew Union College–Jewish Institute of Religion, 1972.
A complete bibliography of sites, arranged alphabetically, containing everything published through 1970 and part of 1971.

For information about specific sites, we now have up-to-date summaries of results (*BRL,*[2] *EAEHL, EJ*) and bibliographies (the items just named plus Vogel). But all these face the rapid obsolescence typical of this dynamic field; to keep up with new and ongoing excavations, one must consult the periodical indexes (*Elenchus, IZBG, OTA*) and *OTBL*. For periodicals, *OTA* is less complete than *Elenchus* or *IZBG* but stays more current. For the critical debate on older excavations (or any other ongoing issue, for that matter), the *Permucite Index* will be invaluable if it can keep up with the publication program it has set for itself, a premise still in doubt at present writing.

For questions that grow out of study of the biblical text—about the nature of the material culture of a period or of a specific object or term—one must be more resourceful. The encyclopedias and dictionaries are good starting places (*BRL,*[2] *EJ, IDB,* and the *Supplément* to the *Dictionnaire de la Bible* of F. Vigouroux); but for recent developments, nothing but patient search through the newer literature, guided by the publication indexes, will avail.

Finally, to keep abreast of new developments, useful syntheses, and the like, the best means are the *OTBL* and *OTA* for the broad perspective and the "Chronique archéologique" of the *Revue Biblique* and "Notes and News" of the *Israel Exploration Journal* for excavation developments. Also see current and preliminary reports under "Primary Reports" above.

EXCURSUS:
EPIGRAPHIC BIBLIOGRAPHY

Since epigraphic finds are of central importance in biblical studies, we include a list of the most recent summaries, all of which provide entrée into the earlier literature.

H. Donner and W. Röllig. *Kanaanäische und Aramäische Inschriften, I: Texte* (3d ed., 1971); *II: Kommentar* (2d ed., 1968); *III: Glossare, Indizes, Tafeln* (2d ed., 1969). Wiesbaden: Harrassowitz.

A complete collection of Northwest Semitic inscriptions (Phoenician, Punic, Moabite, and Aramaic as well as Hebrew) with transcription, translation, glossaries, indexes, facsimiles, bibliography, and other helps.

J. C. L. Gibson. "Inscriptions, Semitic." *Interpreter's Dictionary of the Bible Supplementary Volume*, ed. Keith Crim. Nashville: Abingdon Press, 1976, pp. 429–36.
Bibliography of recent philological and linguistic studies in addition to new inscriptions.

―――. *Textbook of Syrian Semitic Inscriptions I: Hebrew and Moabite Inscriptions* (1971); *II: Aramaic Inscriptions* (1975); *III: Phoenician and Punic Inscriptions* (forthcoming). Oxford: Clarendon Press.
A collection of the most important inscriptions in transliteration and translation with samples of others—seals, stamps, and so on. Study notes, bibliography, indexes.

Lemaire, André. *Inscriptions Hébraïques, I: Les Ostraca*. Littératures Anciennes du Proche-Orient, 9. Paris: Les Éditions du Cerf, 1977.
A study of all Hebrew ostraca (translation, not transliteration) from the period of the monarchy with discussion and bibliography.

Teixidor, Javier. "Bulletin d'épigraphie sémitique," *Syria* (1967–).
Annual summary of all recent publications of Northwest Semitic epigraphic material: Hebrew, Phoenician, Punic, Aramaic, and so on.

Vattioni, F. "I sigilli ebraici," *Biblica* 50 (1969):357–88;
―――, "I sigilli ebraici II," *Augustinianum* 11 (1971):447–54.
―――, "I sigilli ebraici III", *Annali dell' Istituto Orientale di Napoli* 38 (1978): 227–54.
A catalog of published Hebrew seals.

THE USE OF ARCHAEOLOGY IN
BIBLICAL STUDIES

We have thus far discussed the use of archaeological publications in reconstructing the culture of ancient Palestine. Although it is a difficult discipline to master, this use is a fairly straightforward application of the procedures of empirical research. The use of archaeology in biblical studies, however, raises deeper and more complex issues. The Bible, after all, is not simply an interesting ancient document like the *Iliad* or the *Peloponnesian Wars*; it is the sacred scripture of Judaism and Christianity, two living religions that see in the biblical narrative the story of God's relationship with humankind, a story bound up with the history of the people of Israel. Much of this history occurred within the territory of ancient Palestine and, if the biblical records are accurate, ought to have some correlation with archaeological findings. The presence of this religious interest in the study of Palestinian archaeology introduces a complication for some biblical exegetes, a complication due to what may be called the quasi-sacramental nature of archaeology. Let me illustrate with a personal example.

After finishing my undergraduate degree, which included a minor concentration in Greek language and literature, I spent a year in Europe, the high point of which was a visit to Greece and Athens. There I saw for the first time the places and physical remains associated with my reading and study. The experience is still vivid after more than two decades. I stood at the foot of the Acropolis in the orchestra of the theater where the plays of Aeschylus and Euripides were first performed and sat in the actual throne reserved for the priest of Dionysus during the theatrical festival. I wandered into the Agora Museum in the restored stoa of Attalos, and, going from case to case, came to one which contained actual ostraca used by the Athenians in the fifth century B.C. to banish undesirable citizens. In making out the Greek letters on the sherds, I suddenly realized that many of them bore the name of Themistocles, the very Themistocles who had forged the victory of the Greeks over the Persians at the battle of Salamis in 480 B.C. and who was later ostracized by his ungrateful compatriots. On another day I went across the mountains to Delphi and in the midst of that awesome place saw the very stone that the ancient Greeks had regarded as the navel of the earth. These were moments which left me giddy and deeply moved. All the clichés about archaeology—it breathes life into the bones of history, it bridges the gap of centuries—suddenly became more than simple truisms. Despite millennia of intellectual development toward the abstract and the universal, it is still the concrete and the particular, what we can see and touch, that has the most powerful impact upon our imaginations.

If the remains of Greece can have such effect on us, how much more those of Palestine. Here, for the bearers of the Judeo-Christian heritage, are focused not the aesthetic or intellectual questions but the ultimate ones: those of life, death, and the meaning of existence. What person for whom the biblical tradition has any vitality can remain unmoved while blackening his or her fingers with charcoal from the Babylonian destruction of Jerusalem, or viewing a broken slab from Caesarea which bears the inscribed name of Pontius Pilate, or even picking up a potsherd and finding it impressed by a careless thumbprint—a print in all respects like one's own—left by the hand of the potter, dead for more than three thousand years?

As we learn more about the human being as an entity in whom feelings and emotions have as much right to exist as the rational and analytical faculties, we are more willing to admit the existence of such reactions. Archaeological remains have an effect on many people similar to that of the eucharist on many Christians—suddenly the barriers of time and distance are removed and there is an immediate contact with events and persons of long ago and a realization of unity, of belonging, of identity. These emotions, though natural and legitimate, do pose problems for the critical archaeologist and historian whose first task is to reconstruct the past as accurately and objectively as possible. The powerful, quasi-sacramental pull which archaeology exerts can have a strong unconscious effect on the judgment of the researcher, and the first step toward minimizing its effect is to admit its existence. No historian is wholly free of bias or presupposition; we work toward objectivity only by making ourselves aware of our cultural, intellectual, and emotional predispositions.

In the case of Palestinian archaeology, this self-awareness has been slow in coming. Until the founding of the state of Israel with its passionate though usually secular interest in the monuments of the past, the major "consumers" of archaeological news from Palestine have been those religious communities rooted in the Old Testament, especially the Western Christian community. With the rise of interest in preclassical antiquity during the nineteenth century, the search began in Palestine for the concrete remains of the biblical events. The connection between place and event is powerful—witness the continuous flow of religious pilgrims—and there are subtle pressures, personal and communal, at work upon any biblical exegete who seeks to make use of archaeological material. The immediate concern here is not with the often selective and forced use of archaeology by those who believe the Bible to be an inerrant historical record. Rather it is to point to the temptation, manifest in Christian exegete and Israeli secularist alike, to yield too quickly to the desire to see immediate connections between archaeological evidence and the biblical record. A few examples will serve to illustrate.

Perhaps the most common manifestation of this tendency to look for immediate biblical parallels occurs when excavators seek to date Iron-Age destruction layers at their site by attributing them to events recorded in the Bible: the campaign of Shishak early in the reign of Rehoboam, the Aramean incursions of the ninth century B.C. in the north, and other recorded destructions by the Assyrians and Babylonians. Typically, these connections are drawn even though the area excavated represents only a small percentage of the mound and the destruction could have been due to accident and localized in a few adjacent houses. The problem is compounded when others uncritically pick up the excavator's conclusions and use them either to create erroneous chronological synchronisms with other sites or even to argue

63

circularly for the validity of the biblical tradition: the tradition that was the basis for the identification of the destruction is now viewed as "verified" because of the evidence of the destruction.[17]

There is a second problem with this line of reasoning. Evidence rarely turns up to permit a particular destruction to be attributed to a particular biblical agent. If Roman arrowheads are found in the ashes of Masada, one would agree that Josephus's story of Roman destruction is strongly supported. But without some similar link, how, for example, does one connect the Israelites to any of the destruction layers found in Canaanite cities at the end of the Late Bronze Age, the time of the traditional conquest? Palestine at that time was subject to disturbances at the hands of not only the Israelites but also the Sea Peoples, notably the Philistines, who were occupying territory along the coast. Moreover, the Canaanite city-states were quite willing and able to make war on one another. If the biblical list of cities destroyed by Joshua could be correlated site by site with massive destructions at the end of the Late Bronze Age, one could begin to find the probabilities persuasive. But no such correlation exists.[18] To cite some destructions as being caused by Israelites while assuming alternative explanations for sites that do not fit the pattern raises questions of methodological consistency. It also makes one wonder if the complexity of the process by which Israel's ancient stories were preserved and transmitted has been fully appreciated. Even if archaeological data can be correlated with a particular biblical detail, it is not clear how one makes valid deductions either about other historical details or about the entire picture.

Skepticism about the validity of the search for correlations between the results of archaeology and the biblical record has led some to confine the relevance of archaeology for biblical studies to quite narrow tasks. Perhaps the classic representative of this view is Martin Noth.[19] Although Noth had a deep appreciation of the accomplishments of Palestinian archaeology and applauded its development into an independent discipline, he limited its relevance for biblical studies to topographic research, that is, helping to identify modern sites of ancient cities, and to answering broad questions about patterns of settlement and cultural history. Noth even ruled out connecting a particular build-

17. A point well put by J. Maxwell Miller, *The Old Testament and the Historian* (London: SPCK, 1976), pp. 47–48.

18. See most recently J. Maxwell Miller, "The Israelite Occupation of Canaan", *Israelite and Judaean History*, ed. John H. Hayes and J. Maxwell Miller (London: SCM, 1977), pp. 252–62.

19. Martin Noth, *The Old Testament World*, (London: A. & C. Black, 1966), pp. 139–44. In actual practice, Noth made a much wider use of archaeology, as demonstrated by his unfinished commentary on Kings.

ing with historical events unless the building bears some inscription to identify it or the name of the builder, a condition which is rarely fulfilled.

So austere and removed a role for archaeology in the study of the Old Testament is no more satisfying than the mode of making facile and tendentious connections. As our command of Palestine's archaeological history develops, our ability to make valid individual judgments increases and will continue to increase. To try to confine by fiat an increasingly precise instrument to the task of constructing broad backgrounds is futile.

What then is the proper use of archaeology in the interpretation of the Old Testament? This is a question currently under debate, and an adequate answer would require far more space than is available here. Only some general observations may be offered.

Certainly the task of archaeology is not "to prove the Bible true." Those who make such claims usually mean by this that written texts recovered by archaeology have verified some historical statements in the Bible (certainly true), and consequently the biblical statements about God and his dealings with Israel are also true. It takes no expert in logic to see the fallacy of this argument. Although archaeology can sometimes provide independent evidence for the existence of certain places, persons, or events mentioned in the Bible, it can say nothing at all about whether God had anything to do with any of it. That, for the modern believer as well as for the ancient Israelite, is a matter of faith. The Old Testament is a collection of religious documents produced out of a conviction that Yahweh had chosen the nation Israel for a special relationship to him; to look for "proof" of this religious conviction is to misunderstand both the limits of historical evidence and the nature of faith itself.

Since Israel's interest in history was primarily religious and since the Old Testament originated long before the canons of critical history had been formulated, the Bible not surprisingly contains a wide range of different kinds of material, some of which are sober historical records but many of which are not. Although form criticism and tradition history have developed tools to help distinguish among these different materials, no literary technique is infallible.[20] The Old Testament comes to us as the end product of a long process of transmission—oral, redactional, and textual. Despite our best efforts, the Old Testament will always defy complete understanding. Any verdict upon

20. See two previous books in this series: Gene M. Tucker, *Form Criticism of the Old Testament* (Philadelphia: Fortress Press, 1971), and Walter E. Rast, *Tradition History and the Old Testament* (Philadelphia: Fortress Press, 1972).

this verse or that list as reflecting actual history will remain a matter of judgment, not of certainty, a reality that should give pause to anyone who feels tempted to seek in archaeology confirmation of biblical history.

Archaeology in the study of the Old Testament will certainly continue to play the role consigned to it by Noth—topographical research and cultural history. But such a purview is surely too narrow. The more valuable contribution of archaeology is that it provides a different point of view against which to test our interpretation of the documents, a point of view formed and disciplined by close study of materials contemporary with the biblical events. The interpretation of archaeological materials is certainly subjective and suffers from the problems of missing, incomplete, or misleading evidence. But the interpretation of the written documents is subject to the same distortions. Literary interpretation and the principles that guide it must be continually tested, not simply by other literary criteria, but by all data available. Archaeological evidence is valuable precisely because it provides a different *kind* of data from the literary evidence, data of a different order that were not subject to the same problems of redaction and textual transmission that shaped the documents.

Archaeology and the Old Testament must be read in dialogue with one another; neither one can give a comprehensive picture. The archaeological results may suggest a new understanding of the documents; the documents may provide a key to understand the archaeology—there is indeed a kind of circularity. But it is a circularity of conversation and constant revision, both on the basis of better understanding of the text and of new archaeological evidence. It is a rhythm of the construction of models and hypotheses and their relentless testing against the data, of movement from one synthesis to another more satisfactory synthesis, avoiding both the dogmatism of fixed positions and the anarchy of perpetual tentativeness.

IV

The Archaeologist at Work:
The Age of Solomon

In bringing the Bible and archaeology together, one may begin at either end. One may start with the questions that arise from the biblical text critically understood and bring them to the archaeological data: Is there any archaeological evidence of a conquest of all or part of Canaan by the Israelites? What do we know about the standard of living of the common people during the days of the prophets? Was the destruction of Judah by the Babylonians selective or widespread? Or one may begin with a particular find or body of archaeological data and ask how it may enlighten the biblical text: What light do the Arad or Lachish ostraca throw on the development of biblical Hebrew? What does the stratigraphic history of Beer-sheba tell about the formation of the patriarchal traditions connected with that site? What do the so-called "royal-stamp" jar handles tell us about government or commerce in the kingdom of Judah? The process of reasoning and research, which is our primary concern, remains essentially the same, whichever way one goes. Since we are under constraints of space, we shall illustrate by taking an example of the first sort: What can archaeology tell us about the age of Solomon? Narrowing our focus still further, we shall ask (1) How can we date a particular stratum to the time of Solomon? (2) What do we know about the Solomonic royal cities of Hazor, Megiddo, and Gezer? and (3) What do we know about Solomon's capital city, Jerusalem?[1]

1. For full recent syntheses of the archaeology of the age of Solomon, see, e.g., John Bright, *A History of Israel*, rev. ed. (London: SCM, 1972), pp. 206–24; Gaalyah Cornfeld, *Archaeology of the Bible: Book by Book* (A. & C. Black, 1977), pp. 104–12; Harry Thomas Frank, *Bible, Archaeology, and Faith* (Nashville: Abingdon Press, 1971), pp. 136–57; E. W. Heaton, *Solomon's New Men* (London: Thames and Hudson, 1974), pp. 61–96; K. M. Kenyon, *Royal Cities of the Old Testament* (London: Barrie and Jenkins, 1971), pp. 36–70; idem, *The Bible and Recent Archaeology* (London: British Museum Publications, 1978); J. Alberto Soggin, "The Davidic-Solomonic Kingdom", *Israelite and Judaean History*, ed. John H. Hayes and J. Maxwell Miller (London: SCM, 1977), pp. 332–80, esp. pp. 340–43.

FINDING THE STRATA OF SOLOMON

An absolute date for Solomon in the mid-tenth century B.C., based on reliable biblical and other sources, is certain; the remaining differences over the exact length of his reign and the precise date of its close would not affect this conclusion.[2] The task of the biblical archaeologist, therefore, is to reconstruct a picture of life during this period which will help in understanding the biblical narrative. It need scarcely be emphasized to those who have read and absorbed the lessons of the preceding two chapters that identifying and collecting the relevant evidence is not a simple task. Indeed, not a single monument or object has been recovered that can be linked to Solomon with absolute certainty. There is nothing that bears his name or those of David his father or his son Rehoboam. Consequently, our conclusions about the age of Solomon must result from chains of inferences and deductions rather than from immediate correlations.

In order to understand and test the kind of reasoning involved in identifying Solomonic levels, we must trace it step by step from the beginning. To return to the beginning means to open the question of ceramic typology; for, as we have seen, it is the study of pottery that has provided the chronological framework for Palestine.

Any advanced student of Palestinian archaeology could describe some of the chief characteristics of what is generally accepted as pottery of the Solomonic age: the dark red slip with hand burnish; small black dipper juglets with a tall neck and a button base; storejars with tall simple rims; imported black-on-red ware from Cyprus, decorated with lines and circles, and so on. But they might be harder pressed to explain how the pottery of the Solomonic period was so identified.

Although Sir Flinders Petrie demonstrated the principle of ceramic typology with his excavation at Tell el-Ḥesī beginning in 1890, a sense of the overall ceramic history of Palestine was slow in coming. When R. A. S. Macalister, during the first decade of the century, excavated at Gezer, a city mentioned in 1 Kings 9:15–17 as being fortified by Solomon, he was unable to use ceramic typology to correlate any of his finds to the Solomonic era. A few scholars such as Clarence Fisher and Père L.-H. Vincent began to grasp the overall ceramic sequence, but their insights existed only in an oral tradition, based on their personal observation and intuition.

---

2. See for example J. Maxwell Miller, *The Old Testament and the Historian* (London: SPCK, 1976), Chapter II and pp. 79–80.

After the First World War, when control of Palestine passed from Turkey to Great Britain, excavation burgeoned and advances came rapidly, most notably through the work of William F. Albright who conducted four campaigns at Tell Beit Mirsim, a small site in the Judean Shephelah, from 1926 to 1932. For the first time the ceramic history of the country from the middle of the third millennium B.C. to the end of the monarchy was laid out in clear succession, a structure which continues to be refined and modified but which in its essentials has proved sound.[3]

In Stratum B at Tell Beit Mirsim, the second stratum from the top, Albright found three distinct phases which he designated B_1 to B_3, from the earliest to the latest. Except for the final phase, these were represented mostly by grain pits containing debris that had fallen or been thrown into them. A modern stratigrapher, conscious of the possibilities of mixture in such a situation, would hesitate to base far-reaching conclusions on such evidence; but Albright's unparalleled gifts as a ceramic typologist enabled him to detect and discard the intrusions.

The key was the middle phase, B_2. This phase contained the distinctive painted pottery which had long been labeled "Philistine" and which excavations at Beth-shemesh and Ashkelon had already shown to be later than the end of the Late Bronze Age, that is, later than the period when Cypriote and Mycenean pottery had been heavily imported into Palestine.[4] This sequence tallied with information from reliefs of Ramses III in Egypt. These annals, inscribed on the walls of the temple at Medinet Habu, record Ramses's defeat of the Sea Peoples of whom the Philistines were one group, at the borders of Egypt in the early part of the twelfth century B.C. Thus, for reasons that Albright laid out in some detail, Philistine Stratum B_2 at Tell Beit Mirsim—and *a fortiori* its end—would have to fall after this date.[5]

Turning to the end of Stratum B (B_3), Albright drew parallels between the pottery of this phase, in which Philistine pottery had ceased, and that of Stratum IV at Megiddo where another American expedition was working at the same time. It was in Stratum IV at Megiddo that the famous stables were found, dated by the excavators and by

3. See William F. Albright, *The Excavation of Tell Beit Mirsim in Palestine I: The Pottery of the First Three Campaigns*, AASOR XII (New Haven: American Schools of Oriental Research, 1932); *The Excavation of Tell Beit Mirsim IA: The Bronze Age Pottery of the Fourth Campaign*, AASOR XIII (1933), and *The Excavation of Tell Beit Mirsim III: The Iron Age*, AASOR XXI–XXII (1943).

4. Albright, *Tell Beit Mirsim I*, pp. 53–56.

5. Ibid., pp. 56–58.

Albright to the time of Solomon.[6] Furthermore, Albright observed that the pottery of the phase which followed his Stratum B$_3$, that is, Stratum A$_1$, showed characteristics that placed it earlier rather than later among subsequent typological developments; in fact, he had difficulty distinguishing between the pottery of B$_3$ and A$_1$.[7] Thus, if A$_1$ was early in the succeeding period, that is, the ninth century in Albright's judgment, then B$_3$ must be slightly earlier, in the tenth or very early ninth century. Typically, Albright looked for a historical event that could have destroyed Stratum B at Tell Beit Mirsim and concluded that "since there is only one historical invasion with which to reckon between the middle of David's reign (cir. 980) and the invasion of Sennacherib, namely the conquest of Judah by Shishak, in the fifth year of Rehoboam (cir. 920 B.C.), we are on safe grounds in combining the two events."[8] By this line of argument Albright assigned Stratum B$_3$ to the mid-tenth century B.C.—after the disappearance of Philistine influence and before Pharaoh Shishak's invasion in the days of Solomon's successor. Tell Beit Mirsim B$_3$ thus became the reference point for the pottery of the Solomonic period.

Albright's reasoning was impressive, and with minor modifications his outline of this period of the archaeology of Palestine has proved essentially correct; but one can also see that it needed testing at several points. For example, could the distinctive pottery called "Philistine" be associated in fact with the biblical Philistines of the days of the Judges, thus providing the *terminus post quem* for any Solomonic level? Here Albright has been vindicated by numerous finds in Philistia proper and in the border areas of Judah, more than enough evidence to establish both the connection and the sequence.[9] Particularly important were the discoveries of Benjamin Maisler (who has since changed his name to Mazar) at Tell Qasile, a site in the northern suburbs of Tel Aviv. Mazar found two Philistine phases (Strata XII and XI) which together corresponded to Albright's B$_2$. In addition he found a third (Stratum X) which was late Philistine; and all of them preceded Level IX, the stratum that correlated with Tell Beit Mirsim B$_3$.[10] Without the Qasile evidence, one could argue that Tell Beit

6. W. F. Albright, "The American Excavations at Tell Beit Mirsim," *ZAW* 47 (1929): 13; Robert S. Lamon and Geoffrey M. Shipton, *Megiddo I: Seasons of 1925–1934, Strata I–V*, OIP 42 (Chicago: University of Chicago Press, 1939), pp. 59–60.
7. Albright, *Tell Beit Mirsim I*, pp. 78–79.
8. W. F. Albright, *The Archaeology of Palestine and the Bible*, 3d ed. (Cambridge, Mass.: The American Schools of Oriental Research, 1974), p. 106.
9. See, e.g., R. de Vaux, *The Early History of Israel*, trans. David Smith (London: Darton, Longman & Todd, 1978), pp. 503–16.
10. B. Maisler, "The Excavations at Tell Qasile: Preliminary Report," *IEJ* 1 (1950–51):195.

Mirsim B$_3$, though obviously later than the Philistine period, was earlier than David or Solomon and represented a time late in the period of the Judges. But the three Philistine strata at Qasile (Strata XII–X) amply accounted for the period of the Philistines and the Judges, thus pushing Stratum IX to a later time.

The same effect, but from the other end, was created by the later levels at Tell Qasile. For Stratum IX was followed by two distinct strata, VIII and VII, both of which Mazar dated before the Assyrian destruction of 733–32 B.C.[11] The findings from other sites—Samaria and especially Hazor—applied even more pressure to push the Tell Qasile IX–Tell Beit Mirsim B$_3$ horizon upward to an earlier date. (We shall now begin to call this horizon "Solomonic" for short.) At Hazor following the "Solomonic" phase, Yadin and his associates found seven distinct strata or phases, all of which were clearly of the Iron II period and which they argued had to date before the Assyrian invasion of 732 B.C. Three of these phases lay between the "Solomonic" period and a massive destruction, best attributed to the early. ninth century.[12] In short, with the Tell Qasile Philistine strata pressing the "Solomonic" material down and the later Qasile, Samaria, and Hazor strata squeezing up, the pressures equalized in the tenth century, the age of Solomon.

Other elements of Albright's original argument for the date of Tell Beit Mirsim B$_3$, however, have not stood the test of time. One line of his reasoning stressed the similarity of his pottery to that of Stratum IV at Megiddo with its famous stables, long believed to be Solomonic. However, the American Megiddo excavations in general and their Stratum IV in particular have since been subjected to extensive criticism and reworking, in part by Albright himself. Consequently, as we shall see below, the bulk of Stratum IV, in particular the stables, can no longer be called Solomonic. More serious, perhaps, is Albright's assumption that Stratum B$_3$ was destroyed by Pharaoh Shishak at the end of the tenth century. Albright exemplified the tendency described in Chapter III to attribute each destruction of a site to some known historical event (see p. 63 above). But there is no proof of any sort that Tell Beit Mirsim Stratum B$_3$ was destroyed by the Egyptians: the destruction could have been accidental or by some unknown agent

---

11. Ibid., pp. 195–207. A more recent excavation at Tell Qasile has challenged the dating of Maisler (Mazar), raising the date of Stratum VIII to the tenth century: A. Mazar, "Tell Qasile," *EAEHL* IV, p. 974. See also John S. Holladay, Jr., "Of Sherds and Strata: Contributions toward an Understanding of the Archaeology of the Divided Monarchy," *Magnalia Dei: The Mighty Acts of God*, ed. F. M. Cross, W. E. Lemke, and P. D. Miller (Garden City, N.Y.: Doubleday, 1976), p. 275 and Chart 3, p. 270.
12. Yigael Yadin, *Hazor*, The Schweich Lectures of the British Academy, 1970 (Oxford: Oxford University Press, 1972), pp. 142–3 and 200.

at some other date. There is, in fact, serious doubt whether this part of Judah was invaded by Shishak at all.[13] Furthermore, in the light of newer evidence, there is even a tendency to lower the date of the end of Tell Beit Mirsim B_3 from the tenth century to the early ninth, in effect shifting the datum point from which all the calculations have been made![14]

But if Albright's original argument was flawed and if even subsequent evidence which seemed to bear him out is now challenged (see p. 71, note 11), on what sound methodological basis can one continue to assign "Solomonic" pottery and the associated levels of any site to Solomon? The answer, of course, is that one does so with proper caution. Until and unless we find written evidence to link a stratum and its "Solomonic" pottery to the tenth century, the correlation remains a hypothesis, not a historical certainty. But, this being said, one should not have the impression that we are floating on a pond of subjective opinion. Even if some strands are pulled from the argument, including some which Albright adduced to *define* "Solomonic" pottery in the first place, the total garment does not come unraveled. There is enough cumulative stratigraphic evidence, such as that from Hazor and the unpublished materials from the new excavations at Gezer, to make our attribution of "Solomonic" pottery to the tenth century far and away the *best current hypothesis,* the one that most competent observers expect will stand the test of time. To remain suspended in skepticism until there is absolute certainty is to reveal a lack of awareness of the empirical nature of archaeological data and how ongoing discovery and debate continually shape the data into systems that are then further tested and refined.

Moreover, to assign a stratum to the Solomonic period or to any other, one looks for overlapping lines of argument. Here, for example, is the way Yadin phrases his conclusions regarding the "Solomonic" levels of Hazor:

The identification of Stratum X with Solomon's city was obtained as a result of many factors: the stratigraphy, which showed Stratum X to be the first Iron Age city above the remains of Stratum XII (and XI in Area B), but below the monumental remains of Stratum VIII (ninth century); the pottery, which was identical with other tenth-century strata in other excavated Tells, and above all the biblical passage (I Kings 9:15) which states that Hazor was built by Solomon together with Gezer and Megiddo.

13. For a recent discussion of the Shishak incursion, see K. A. Kitchen, *The Third Intermediate Period in Egypt (1100–650 B.C.)* (Warminster: Aris and Phillips, 1973), pp. 432–47 and the earlier literature cited there.
14. Y. Aharoni and Ruth Amiran, "A New Scheme for the Sub-Division of the Iron Age in Palestine," *IEJ* 8 (1958):182; Holladay, "Of Sherds and Strata," Chart 3, p. 271.

The discovery of a city-gate . . . identical in plan with the Solomonic gate at Megiddo . . . clinched the identification of Stratum X as representing the Hazor of Solomon's time.[15]

In short, in the case of the "Solomonic" era as in any other, ceramic evidence, albeit the main chronological indicator, is not the only one. There are other lines of argument, as we shall see shortly, which have contributed to the consensus about the identification of the Solomonic levels, a consensus which we shall honor hereafter by deleting those quotation marks of tentativeness around the phrase Solomonic era.

HAZOR, MEGIDDO, AND GEZER

In the summary of his arguments for the Solomonic date of Stratum XB at Hazor just quoted, Yadin tied Hazor to the sites of Megiddo and Gezer, referring to the passage from 1 Kings 9:15–17 to which we have already alluded. These verses are part of a section which deals with Solomon's use of forced labor to do his building projects. The crucial portion reads as follows:

This is the account of the forced labor which King Solomon raised in order to build the temple of Yahweh, his own residence, the Millo [the supporting platform?], and the wall of Jerusalem, Hazor, Megiddo, and Gezer. Pharaoh, king of Egypt, had besieged and captured Gezer, burning it and killing the Canaanites who lived in the city, and had given it as dowry to his daughter, who was Solomon's wife. So Solomon rebuilt Gezer. . . . (Author's translation)

Although this passage mentions a fourth city, Jerusalem, we shall reserve it for later and look now at the three outlying sites of Hazor, Megiddo, and Gezer, all of which have been extensively investigated.

Gezer was the first site in Palestine to undergo excavation on a large scale. In this early effort during the first decade of the twentieth century, Macalister, the excavator, could identify nothing with certainty as dating from the Solomonic period. He did find some square towers inserted into the city walls, towers with corners that had been reinforced with blocks of finely cut ashlar. When the German excavator Schumacher, who was then digging at Megiddo, visited Gezer one day, he remarked that the ashlar blocks resembled stonework in one of his buildings which he thought was Solomonic. After seeing some photographs of the Megiddo structures, Macalister was persuaded by the similarities and suggested that the Gezer towers had been added by Solomon.[16] Schumacher had no solid evidence for the historical context of his finds at Megiddo; at least if he did, he kept it to himself,

15. Yadin, Hazor, p. 135.
16. R. A. S. Macalister, The Excavations of Gezer, 1902–05 and 1907–09 (London: Committee of the Palestine Exploration Fund, 1912), I, pp. 255–56.

for his final publication simply presents the finds as cultural layers, detached from historical considerations.[17] In reality, the reasoning of Schumacher and Macalister was little better than a guess: the Bible says that Solomon carried out construction at Gezer and Megiddo; ashlar masonry is rare and looks expensive; therefore, the ashlar masonry represents Solomon's buildings. Despite the manifest weakness of this syllogism—a bit caricatured, to be sure—one should not feel too superior; given the limited data, it was at least a possible hypothesis. It would be tested by new information as it appeared; but the rhythm of hypothetical synthesis–new data–revised hypothetical synthesis is precisely how archaeological reasoning proceeds.

By the mid-1920s things began to sort themselves out a bit. When an American expedition returned to Megiddo in 1925, sponsored by the Oriental Institute of the University of Chicago and supported by substantial grants of Rockefeller money, Albright was at work at Tell Beit Mirsim; and the ceramic history of the country was becoming clearer. Nevertheless, as we shall see, the arguments advanced by the Megiddo staff to identify their "Solomonic" level were still based largely on circumstantial evidence rather than methodological advances.

The candidate of the Chicago team for the Solomonic level was Stratum IV, numbering from the top.[18] The original strategy of the expedition had been to uncover and remove each stratum across the entire top of the mound. The goal was soon abandoned but not before Stratum IV had been almost entirely exposed (Fig. 7). Very few domestic houses were found. Instead this stratum consisted for the most part of large public buildings surrounded by a stout city wall built with alternating offsets and insets. This wall, wall 325, was some 3.6 meters in thickness (nearly 12 ft.).

Of most interest were four structures interpreted by the excavators as stables.[19] Each building contained a number of units composed of a central aisle separated from two side aisles by rows of stone pillars. The central aisle was floored with lime plaster and the other two with rubble. Through one corner of some pillars a tethering hole had been bored, and frequently between the pillars were found blocks hollowed out on top in the form of a manger. The southern complex 1576 included a large courtyard with sheds along one side which could have provided garage space for chariots.

Other elements of Stratum IV included two imposing buildings,

17. G. Schumacher, *Tell el-Mutesellim I* (Leipzig: Rudolph Haupt, 1908).

18. *Megiddo I*, pp. 8–61. Note that stratum numbers were changed in the interim between the preliminary and final reports, a common occurrence (p. xxvii).

19. Ibid., pp. 32–47.

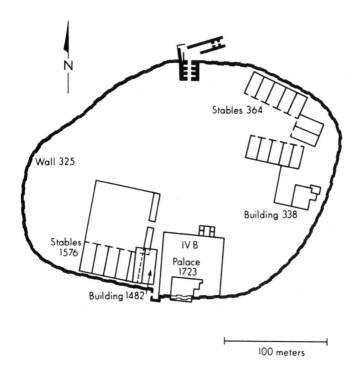

FIG. 7. STRATUM IV AT MEGIDDO

each set in a courtyard paved with lime plaster. On the eastern side
of the mound was building 338, which was interpreted by the writers
of the final report volume as a governmental headquarters.[20] Another
palatial building, 1723, was found in the southern part of the mound
just east of the southern stable complex. Imposingly sited in a wide
plastered courtyard, it was approached through its own gate tower.
However, palace 1723 had clearly preceded the main phase of Stratum
IV since wall 325 was built over it. Yet for reasons which the report
makes clear, 1723 did not belong to the next major phase below,
Stratum V; and so for palace 1723 and adjacent building 1482 the
excavators proposed an intermediate phase between V and IV which
they called IVB.[21]

---

20. Ibid., pp. 58–59. Note the references on p. 58 to the internal debate within the
Megiddo staff about the use of the building. In fact, in an earlier volume of the Megiddo
series, May treats the structure as a temple: H. G. May, *Material Remains of the
Megiddo Cult*, OIP 26 (Chicago: University of Chicago Press, 1935).
21. *Megiddo I*, pp. 11–27.

The arguments to connect this Stratum IV with the age of Solomon were circumstantial but not unimpressive.[22] Assuming that 1 Kings 9:15 is correct, one of the Iron-Age strata at Megiddo should produce structures that would be royal in size and expensive in building technique. The buildings of Stratum IV certainly fulfilled these expectations. They were clearly part of a single plan carried out over the entire surface of the mound, too massive to be private in origin. The quality of their construction was excellent: well-cut ashlar stones, very rare in pre-Roman Palestinian sites, were found throughout Stratum IV, especially at corners of buildings and at intervals in piers to reinforce sections of more ordinary fieldstones. Only the royal structures at Samaria, nearly a century later than Solomon but clearly related in concept, provided an apt parallel. Also suggestive of royal or governmental grandeur were a number of carved proto-Ionic capitals (now more commonly called proto-Aeolic) found near building 338 and further south near the gateway which led into the courtyard of palace 1723. Furthermore, P. L. O. Guy, one of the excavators of building 338, found evidence for a construction technique which was apparently the same as the one described in 1 Kings 6:36 (Eng.) and 7:12. These passages state that in building the inner courtyard of the Jerusalem temple, Solomon's craftsmen laid three rows of ashlar stones which they then topped with a course of cedar beams, possibly a technique to stabilize the building against earthquake. Wherever the foundation walls of building 338 survived to their original height, there were indeed three courses. The top course always showed signs of burning, indicating that the third course was overlain by some combustible material. Moreover, in the courtyard outside the west wall of building 338 a chunk of charcoal turned up which botanists in England were able to identify as cedar.[23]

Finally, if 1 Kings 9:15 demanded a Solomonic level at Megiddo, verse 19 appeared to clinch the identification, for it spoke of cities built by Solomon for his chariots and horsemen. According to the reconstructions of the excavators, the massive stable complexes would have comprised seventeen units in four separate buildings, providing room for 450 horses, certainly a project worthy of Israel's richest king. Pottery, it will be noted, played little part in the argument of the Megiddo report; Lamon and Shipton simply noted the similarities

22. Ibid., pp. 59–61.
23. P. L. O. Guy, *New Light from Armageddon: Second Provisional Report (1927–29) on the Excavations at Megiddo in Palestine*, OIC 9 (Chicago: University of Chicago Press, 1931), pp. 34–35.

between Stratum IV forms and Albright's B$_3$ at Tell Beit Mirsim, but they attempted no close analysis.

One bothersome problem in attributing Stratum IV to Solomon remained unresolved, namely, Stratum IVB, composed of palace 1723 with its courtyard and gate and the associated building 1482. Stratigraphically these structures had to be earlier than the main part of Stratum IV. Foundation walls of part of building 1482 extended under the southern stable complex 1576, and city wall 325 of Stratum IV proper was built right across the southern part of palace 1723 which obviously no longer existed in the main period of Stratum IV (Fig. 7). But if Solomon had built Stratum IV, who built IVB? If Solomon had hired Phoenician craftsmen to construct the temple in Jerusalem (1 Kings 5:18—Eng.), one could assume that the excellent stonework of Stratum IV derived from that same source.[24] But the craftsmanship of Stratum IVB was equally excellent, quite unlike the typical Israelite fieldstone construction. Lamon and Shipton were not sure how to resolve the problem. Perhaps palace 1723 and its walled courtyard had been built by David as an isolated outpost. Or, more likely in their view, IVB represented an early stage in the Solomonic building program which was later abandoned when a more ambitious nationwide strategy of fortifications was inaugurated.[25]

The arguments of the Megiddo staff for the Solomonic date of Stratum IV, however impressive, were immediately challenged; indeed they are methodologically weak. Archaeology is an empirical discipline and its arguments must be rooted in stratigraphy and typology; circumstantial and rational arguments are insufficient. Although the Megiddo methods of excavation and publication represented in many ways the best then available, they were nevertheless inadequate to recover and present those essential pieces of information that could have settled the issue. We can illustrate with a few examples.

In a prescient review of *Megiddo I*, J. W. Crowfoot proposed an alternative reconstruction.[26] He had just finished a dig at Samaria which had further explored the palace and acropolis walls built by Omri and Ahab in the ninth century B.C. Crowfoot was struck by the typological similarities of the ashlar masonry at Samaria and that in the Stratum IV structures at Megiddo, not only in the shape and size

---

24. Yigal Shiloh has recently reexamined all the evidence for early ashlar masonry in Israel and has raised serious questions about the prevailing assumption that it is Phoenician in origin: *The Proto-Aeolic Capital and Israelite Ashlar Masonry*, Qedem 11 (Jerusalem: Institute of Archaeology, Hebrew University, 1979).
25. *Megiddo I*, p. 59.
26. J. W. Crowfoot, "Megiddo—A Review," *PEQ* 72 (1940):132–47.

of the stones but in the way they were laid. Moreover, both sites had produced proto-Aeolic capitals of identical design. As for the stables, they could as easily be attributed to Ahab as to Solomon. After all, Ahab was famous for his chariotry: in the inscriptions of Shalmaneser III, he is reported to have commanded 2000 chariots in a battle against Assyria at Qarqar.[27] The passage in 1 Kings 9:15–19, cited by the Megiddo excavators, does not say that Megiddo was built by Solomon as a chariot city; indeed this reference seems to belong to a different category at the end of that passage. For these and other reasons, Crowfoot proposed that the Solomonic stratum at Megiddo was in fact Stratum V and that Stratum IV with its stables and city wall should be credited to Ahab.

Albright also was not happy with the Megiddo report, although for different reasons. With his unmatched knowledge of the pottery chronology, he could not agree with Crowfoot that Stratum V was the Solomonic age: the pottery was too early.[28] But he was troubled by the in-between Stratum IVB with its palace 1723, a phase which the excavators had proposed was a false start for the Solomonic building program. Reading the report carefully, Albright spotted evidence that Stratum IVB was not confined, as the excavators had thought, to the southern quarter. Rather, there were at least two buildings in the eastern part of the mound that were built over Stratum V but before city wall 325 of Stratum IV, that is, in the same intermediate position as palace 1723.[29] A detailed examination of the pottery from those two buildings by Albright's student, G. Ernest Wright, convinced both of them that the vessels found in these buildings were indeed earlier than the main corpus of Stratum IV and should be attributed to the mid-tenth century. Thus Albright proposed that the Solomonic level proper was Stratum IVB, not Stratum IV as a whole, and that the offsets–insets wall around the mound had been built after the raid of Pharaoh Shishak, a part of whose triumphal stele had been found in one of Schumacher's dumps. It is curious in hindsight that Albright did not take the next logical step and question the Solomonic date of the great stable complexes since the southern one was also built over structures of Stratum IVB. But he had accepted them as Solomonic from the time of their discovery and did not see cause to change his mind.

---

27. Trans. A. Leo Oppenheim, *Ancient Near Eastern Texts Relating to the Old Testament*, ed. James B. Pritchard, 2d ed. (Princeton: Princeton University Press, 1955), p. 279.
28. *Tell Beit Mirsim III*, pp. 2–3, n. 1.
29. Ibid., p. 29, n. 10.

Let us pause briefly to look at the kinds of arguments used both by the Megiddo staff and the critics. The reasoning of Lamon and Shipton is almost entirely circumstantial: the pottery of Stratum IV falls roughly into the time period of Solomon; therefore, given the biblical references and the fine quality of the buildings and masonry, the level must be Solomonic. Reduced to its simplest terms, their argument has surprisingly little foundation in hard evidence. Crowfoot's case is also partly circumstantial, although admittedly the biblical text of 1 Kings 9:15–19 is sufficiently imprecise that it could reflect a historical reality underlying either Crowfoot's theory or that of the excavators. But Crowfoot's argument is also partly typological: the masonry of Megiddo IV was indeed remarkably similar in more than one way to the ninth-century work at Samaria. Such an argument, however, is methodologically problematic: two examples are not sufficient evidence to demonstrate either direction or speed of the development of a type. Would royal masonry change discernibly in seventy-five years? The evidential base at that point was simply too small to tell.[30] Albright's arguments, not all of which are presented here, were in part circumstantial but mostly stratigraphic and typological—how structures, phases, and pottery interrelate. Because of the way that Megiddo was dug and published, however, such information is not easy to extract. None of the plans of Stratum IV is supplied with reduced elevations. Only structures, not earth layers, were assigned locus numbers. Pottery not found inside a structure is described as found "near" a locus or "off to one side," descriptions which are stratigraphically useless.[31] Those who try to use the Megiddo volumes to establish stratigraphic relationships of pottery types have to work case by case, making a critical evaluation of every single find spot. In short, despite the enormous expenditure of time and money represented in the Megiddo report, the evidence needed to answer simple stratigraphic questions is often missing. One or two sections cut from the stables through the fortifications and properly drawn and published could have resolved problems which even now are not entirely clear.

30. Kathleen Kenyon's writings on the problems of Samaria and Megiddo illustrate the dangers of drawing conclusions from too small a typological sample. In her original comparison of the sites, she adopted Crowfoot's arguments based on the similarity of the masonry and used them to argue for a mid-ninth-century date for Megiddo IVB: J. W. Crowfoot, G. M. Crowfoot, and K. M. Kenyon, *Samaria–Sebaste III: The Objects from Samaria* (London: Palestine Exploration Fund, 1957), pp. 200–201. Later when, as we shall see below, Yadin established the Solomonic date of IVB on firmer grounds, Kenyon was forced to withdraw her argument based on the masonry and concede that the similarities between Megiddo and Samaria could be due simply to the use of Phoenician masons by both Solomon and Omri: *Archaeology in the Holy Land*, 3d ed. (London: Ernest Benn, 1970), pp. 346–7.
31. *Megiddo I*, p. xxiv.

But to come back to Solomonic Megiddo. Excavation of the city gate of Stratum IV had been completed too late to be published in *Megiddo I*, and so the full picture of the "Solomonic" stratum was deferred until *Megiddo II* appeared in 1948.[32] This gate, at the north edge of the mound, proved to be a magnificent structure of unique design (Figs. 7 and 8A). The main inner gate had four piers forming three opposing bays on either side of the passage. Evidently only the outer pair of piers had sockets for a door, indicating that the other bays were left free for the many activities that the Old Testament describes as occurring in the gate of the city (for example, Ruth 4:1). As in all ancient gates, the passageway and bays were roofed to form a strong defensive tower (see 2 Sam. 18:24). Going out of the city through this four-entry gate, one entered a walled courtyard which sloped down to the right to a second smaller gate with only two piers, through which one reached the outside. The total massive complex was very well built, with generous use of the fine ashlar stones so familiar from other buildings in this stratum.

Few doubted the attribution of this gate to the Solomonic period, although all arguments were circumstantial. Albright, for example, pointed out that the four-entry design paralleled Ezekiel's description of the gates in the Jerusalem temple (Ezek. 40:5–16), gates that of course had originally been built by Solomon.[33] But to attribute this gate to the main phase of Stratum IV as defined by the excavators created problems, for superimposed on the four-entry gate of Stratum IV were two other gates, one with three piers and one above that with two. Both of these the excavators had assigned to Stratum III, arguing that the three-entry gate had never been completed but had been abandoned and supplanted by the gate with two piers.[34] This problematic explanation was challenged by Wright who had been asked to review the new Megiddo report for the *Journal of the American Oriental Society*. Building on the observation that the intermediate Stratum IVB was not confined to palace 1723 and the southern part of the mound, Wright noted that in the northern gate area and nearby structures, the excavators had proposed two phases of Stratum V, namely VB and VA, although they were unable to isolate these phases convincingly anywhere else on the mound. Wright saw immediately that this represented the same situation as in the south with palace 1723,

32. *Megiddo II: Seasons of 1935–39*, by the Megiddo Expedition, Gordon Loud, Field Director, OIP 62 (Chicago: University of Chicago Press, 1948), pp. 46–57.
33. W. F. Albright, Review of *Megiddo II*, AJA 53 (1949):215. His suggestion was further worked out by his student Carl Gordon Howie: "The East Gate of Ezekiel's Temple Enclosure and the Solomonic Gateway of Megiddo," BASOR 117 (1950):13–19.
34. *Megiddo I*, p. 74.

that is, an intermediate phase between the main phases of Stratum V and IV. But the excavators had subdivided Stratum IV in one instance, and Stratum V in the other, thus:

Gate area		Southern area
IV		IV
VA	←——— intermediate ———→	IVB
VB		V

Wright then examined the pottery attributed to Stratum VA and VB in the gate area and was convinced that the former was identical to the pottery from buildings 10 and 51 that Albright had already added to the "intermediate stratum."[35] The latter group of pottery was no different from what the excavators had called simply Stratum V elsewhere. Hence, Wright argued, Stratum VA in the gate area should be combined with IVB. This done, the problem of the surplus gate is resolved. For if the Solomonic stratum is VA–IVB, then the four-entry gate is the only candidate for its city gate. This gate was probably heavily damaged at the time of the Shishak raid and replaced by the three-entry gate which would then have served for the balance of Stratum IV. Finally, the two-entry gate would then fit naturally with Stratum III, a more reasonable solution.[36]

The designation of Stratum VA–IVB at Megiddo as Solomonic was convincing to many, though by no means to all. From her independent examination of the pottery, Kathleen Kenyon insisted that the Solomonic stratum would have to be V and that IVB could not have been founded before the middle of the succeeding century.[37] She did not exclude the possibility that the four-entry gate could be Solomonic, though there was no hard evidence. Moreover, even Wright and Albright disagreed on the date of the offsets–insets wall: Wright attributed it to Solomon[38] but Albright dated it to the end of the century.[39] These differences among eminent scholars are troubling to

---

35. G. Ernest Wright, Review of *Megiddo II*, *JAOS* 70 (1950):59.

36. G. Ernest Wright, "The Discoveries at Megiddo, 1935–39," *BA* 13 (1950):42–44. Recent investigation into the archives of the Oriental Institute has turned up evidence that the Chicago excavators were themselves aware of an early structural stage in the gate of Stratum IV and even referred to it as IVB. For some reason, however, they chose to interpret it as an "impractical" early phase, not a phase of active use. See Yigal Shiloh, "Solomon's Gate at Megiddo as Recorded by Its Excavator, R. Lamon, Chicago," *Levant* 12 (1980):69–76.

37. *Samaria–Sebaste III*, p. 203; Kathleen M. Kenyon, *Archaeology in the Holy Land* (London: Ernest Benn, 1960), pp. 248 and 269–71.

38. G. Ernest Wright, *Biblical Archaeology* (Philadelphia: Westminster Press and London: Gerald Duckworth, 1957), p. 132.

39. *Tell Beit Mirsim III*, p. 18, n. 6.

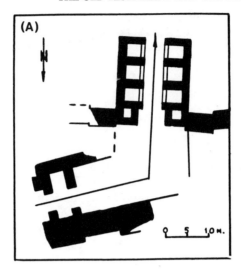

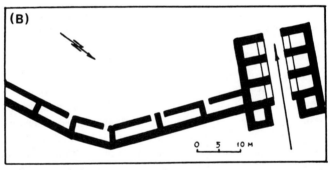

FIG. 8. SOLOMONIC GATES AT MEGIDDO (A) AND HAZOR (B)

nonspecialists who are looking for unambiguous results, but they are inevitable, given not only the frequent inadequacy of the raw data, in this case the Megiddo publications, but also differing presuppositions, points of view, levels of knowledge, soundness of judgment, and so on. It becomes easier to understand how some of the most "assured results" of the relation of archaeology to the Bible get overturned, as was eventually to happen in the case of Megiddo.

To explain how the Megiddo evidence was reinterpreted, we must turn to the third of the royal cities of Solomon, namely Hazor.

Apart from some minor soundings in the late 1920s, Hazor's excavations date to the 1950s with an additional season in 1968. They were the first major undertakings of the archaeological scholars of the new state of Israel, led by Yigael Yadin who had returned to an archaeo-logical career after serving as a general in the Israeli army.

That Stratum X at Hazor is the Solomonic level seems clear, al-though it must be admitted that the final report on that stratum has never appeared.[40] Like Megiddo, Solomon's Hazor was a new city al-though much smaller in size, only 6.5 acres, crowded into the tri-angular western half of the upper tell and surrounded with a casemate wall (a double wall divided into sections by partitions: see Fig. 8B). The structures uncovered inside the walls were few—perhaps a bar-racks near the city gate and a fortress or citadel at the most inaccessi-ble point on the western end. Far and away the most interesting structure was the city gate, for it turned out to be nearly identical in plan to the Stratum IV (or VA–IVB) gate at Megiddo. In fact, the Hazor gate differed significantly in only two ways: the amount of ashlar stones used by the Hazor builders was apparently much less, and there was no outer two-pier gate. To be sure, the area outside the gate was not explored and may yet produce such a structure. The strong similarity of the two gates suggested to Yadin that they must be contemporary. Since the cumulative evidence for a tenth-century date for the Hazor X gate was convincing (see the section above on pot-tery), Hazor could now provide the necessary context for the Megiddo gate which had been typologically unique and stratigraphically uncer-tain. A Solomonic date for the Megiddo gate thus became much more likely.

The discovery of this second four-entry gate at Hazor sparked Yadin to one of the nicest pieces of detective work in the annals of Palestinian archaeology. It will be remembered that Hazor was the third of the cities of the list in 1 Kings 9:15–17 to be excavated, Gezer and Megiddo being the others. Although Macalister had turned over nearly half the mound at Gezer and had traced the city walls around most of the site, he was able to suggest only some secondary towers in the city walls as possible Solomonic remains. In light of the new information from Hazor, Yadin went back to Macalister's final report and, paging carefully through it, came to a drawing which immediately caught his eye (Fig. 9).[41] The drawing, labeled a "Maccabean castle," repre-sented structures which Macalister had dated to the second century

40. Yadin published a detailed preliminary report as part of the Schweich Lectures of 1970: *Hazor* (Oxford: Oxford University Press, 1972), Chapter XII. But only the plates of the final report on the last two seasons have been published, not the volume of descriptive text or plans: Yigael Yadin et al., *Hazor III–IV: An Account of the Third and Fourth Seasons of Excavations*, 1957–8 (Jerusalem: Magnes Press, 1961).
41. Y. Yadin, "Solomon's City Wall and Gate at Gezer," *IEJ* 8 (1958):80–86; Macalis-ter, *The Excavation of Gezer*, I, p. 217.

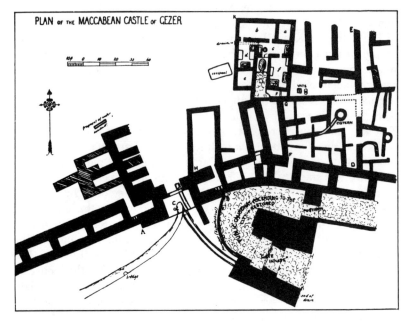

FIG. 9. MACALISTER'S "MACCABEAN CASTLE" AT GEZER

B.C. But in the hodgepodge of walls, Yadin spotted several striking elements: a casemate wall running from west to east, an outer structure with two piers, similar to the outer gate at Megiddo, and the western half of what appeared to be a four-entry gate. With the other elements of Macalister's plan removed and the eastern half of the gate restored (Fig. 10), the similarities to the Hazor and Megiddo gates, especially the latter, are startling. In fact, the measurements of the Hazor, Megiddo, and—as best Yadin could judge—Gezer gates and walls were so similar that Yadin proposed that all had been built by the same architect.

Yadin had based his reasoning on Macalister's plans alone, but empirical support was soon to come. In 1964 a new archaeological project took the field at Gezer with a test of Yadin's hypothesis as one of its objectives. Macalister had reburied the "castle" in order to protect it from a local population in search of building stone, and so there was no trace of its presence on the surface. However, a bit to the west, a portion of what was rightly judged to be part of the casemate wall protruded from the ground, and work began there. Results came quickly. Surfaces just inside the wall yielded the characteristic red

84

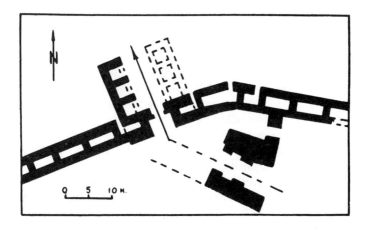

FIG. 10. YADIN'S RECONSTRUCTION OF THE GEZER GATE

burnished wares of the late-tenth century, indicating that the wall had been built sometime before that. Furthermore, since the debris immediately under the wall produced pottery that could not be much earlier than the mid-tenth century, a date for the wall in the mid to late-tenth century was assured, that is, the Solomonic period.[42]

A major effort to reexcavate the "castle" was now clearly justified. After rapid removal of the dumps over the site, the four western piers were apparent. But covering the eastern half of the gate were the angled structures—indeed Hellenistic in date—which had led Macalister to date the whole to the second century B.C. Would there be any trace remaining of the eastern piers, or had they been removed in the Hellenistic reconstruction? To shorten the story of several seasons of patient excavation, the eastern half was indeed intact, and the now familiar four-entry pattern totally apparent (see Frontispiece A). As expected, the pottery from the founding phase of the gate pointed to a mid-tenth-century date. The outer two-entry gate was not reexcavated, but the similarities to Megiddo make it almost certain that the layout at Gezer was identical to that at Megiddo, only in mirror image. Moreover, in the final season of the new excavations, J. D. Seger found one of the reinforcing towers that Macalister had guessed to be Solomonic and excavated against the foundations. Again, the latest pottery was from the early tenth century, evidence that Macalister's

42. William G. Dever, "Excavations at Gezer," BA 30 (1967):61; W. G. Dever, H. D. Lance, and G. E. Wright, Gezer I: Preliminary Report of the 1964–66 Seasons (Jerusalem: Hebrew Union College Biblical and Archaeological School, 1970), p. 63.

intuition had been correct: the towers with their ashlar corners were indeed Solomonic.[43]

Meanwhile, Yadin's line of investigation had led him inevitably back to Megiddo. Both Hazor and Gezer suggested that there might well be a typological connection between four-entry gates and casemate walls. Of the three cities, only Megiddo did not fit the pattern, at least if the excavators had been correct in associating the four-entry gate with the solid offsets–insets wall 325. But, Yadin asked, were they correct?

Once the proper question had been framed, finding the answer on the site was ridiculously easy. Exploring the circumference of the offsets–insets wall, Yadin found a place to the east of the gate where it was still intact, overlying a long, unexplained stretch of ashlar masonry. In a three-day excavation in January of 1960, Yadin moved a few stones and together with his architect, Immanuel Dunayevsky, solved a problem that had vexed scholars for over twenty years. He found that the ashlar stones were the outside wall of a large structure, similar to palace 1723 in the southern part of the mound and stratigraphically identical, that is, under the offsets–insets wall and above Stratum V structures. Second, the walls of this palace (palace 6000 as it was later called) ran *under* the northern stable complex! Finally, and perhaps most gratifying, Yadin found a number of whole or partial casemate chambers running both east and west from the sides of the palace, forming a clear section of casemate wall.[44]

These results, obtained with so little effort, revolutionized the understanding of Megiddo IV. In the first place, Crowfoot and Albright had been right: the solid wall was not Solomonic but later, doubtless part of a reconstruction of the site in the ninth century. Also the famous Megiddo stables, which had been labeled Solomonic in so many popular histories and handbooks, were therefore also later; for they were clearly earlier than palace 6000 and contemporary with the solid wall.[45] The intermediate Stratum VA–IVB now emerged as an important

---

43. J. D. Seger, "Tel Gezer," *IEJ* 24 (1974):134. Kenyon failed to take this evidence into account and wanted to date both the towers and the wall into which they are set to the Hellenistic period: K. M. Kenyon, Review of *Gezer II*, *PEQ* 109 (1977):57. See also her *Archaeology in the Holy Land*, 4th ed. (London: Ernest Benn; and New York: W. W. Norton, 1979), p. 251.

44. Y. Yadin, "New Light on Solomon's Megiddo," *BA* 23 (1960):62–68. For a summary of all the new work at Megiddo, see Yadin, *Hazor* (1972), pp. 150–64.

45. Since Yadin's work has removed the "stables" from the Solomonic period, they are of no further concern here. However, it should be noted that the identification of these buildings as stables has now been challenged by James B. Pritchard in "The Megiddo Stables: A Reassessment," *Near Eastern Archaeology in the Twentieth Century*, ed. James A. Sanders (Garden City, N.Y.: Doubleday, 1970), pp. 268–76. See also Zeev Herzog, "The Storehouses," *Beer-sheba I: Excavations at Tel Beer-sheba, 1969–71 Seasons*, ed. Yohanan Aharoni, Publications of the Institute of Archaeology 2 (Tel Aviv: Tel Aviv University, 1973), pp. 23–30. For a defense of the traditional interpretation, see Y. Yadin, "The Megiddo Stables," *Magnalia Dei: The Mighty Acts of God*, ed. F. M.

stratum in its own right, comprising the southern palace 1723 with adjoining building 1482, the new palace 6000, the buildings which Albright and Wright had previously identified, and the casemate wall (Fig. 11). In two other short seasons, Yadin found traces of an impor-

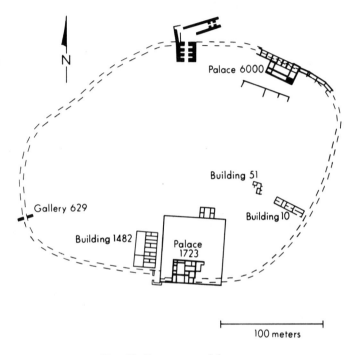

FIG. 11. SOLOMONIC MEGIDDO

tant building just south of palace 6000, plus evidence that ashlar-built gallery 629 which gave access to the water supply was also Solomonic. Because the city wall between the newly found casemates and the four-entry gate had been removed in previous excavations, Yadin could not prove that the casemate wall and the gate were connected stratigraphically; but the similarity of the situations at Hazor and Gezer

Cross, W. E. Lemke, and P. D. Miller, Jr. (Garden City, N.Y.: Doubleday, 1976), pp. 249–52. A definitive study of the question by John S. Holladay, Jr., is forthcoming in *The Archaeology of Jordan and Other Studies Presented to S. H. Horn*, ed. L. T. Geraty. Another element originally assigned to Stratum IV that now appears to be post-Solomonic is building 338 (see Fig. 7). Its ashlar stones are probably reused from the VB–IVA level. Also the courtyard wall around palace 1723 is secondary in its surviving form, but it probably replaced walls on the same lines dating from the original Solomonic phase.

has persuaded most that the four-entry gate at Megiddo is also part of the Solomonic stratum.[46]

Let us come back to our starting point, 1 Kings 9:15-17, and summarize what eighty years of investigation and debate have concluded about the Solomonic cities of Hazor, Megiddo, and Gezer. First, however, since our concern is primarily methodological, let us review the factors that must shape our conclusions.

The realities that encourage caution are at least three: (1) No stratum identified as Solomonic has produced written evidence for that equation. The identifications are based on converging lines of different kinds of evidence, primarily the stratigraphic sequences, the ceramic typology based in stratigraphy, and inferences from the written records, mainly the Bible itself. (2) The excavation of all three cities at the Solomonic level was only partial, even at Megiddo. The resulting picture therefore is doubtless skewed. For example, all three sites have yielded mostly large governmental or military structures. We know next to nothing about the houses or ordinary structures of the period at these sites. (3) The reconstruction of Solomonic Stratum VA–IVB at Megiddo is largely inferential, based on a critical reworking of the published material plus the results of Yadin's narrowly targeted digs. The resulting reconstruction may be the best explanation of the evidence *as published,* but the very imprecisions in the original excavation and publication which necessitated the reworking render the conclusions uncertain. In addition, Yadin's far-reaching revisions are supported only by preliminary reports; the detailed final report has yet to appear.

Although these factors counsel caution, they do not counsel despair. The converging arguments of stratigraphy and typology may be refined in detail as more data accrue, but the possibility of a major error is remote. If these strata of Hazor, Megiddo, and Gezer are not to be attributed to Solomon, they must nevertheless represent major governmental structures of the mid-tenth century B.C. To refuse to make the connection between them and the government which we know to have been in power in the mid-tenth century is to pretend that archaeology can contribute to the writing of history only when absolute certainty is reached. But most modern historians are aware of the limitations of all the different kinds of historical evidence and reject as an illusion the attainment of "absolute certainty." They are willing to settle for

46. The late Yohanan Aharoni remained unconvinced that Yadin had in fact found a casemate wall at Megiddo and strongly defended the Solomonic date of the solid offsets–insets wall. See his article "The Stratification of Israelite Megiddo," *JNES* 31 (1972): 302–11; also Yadin's sharp reply: "A Note on the Stratigraphy of Israelite Megiddo," *JNES* 32 (1973):330.

the best current hypothesis, which in this case would certainly be that these strata are Solomonic in origin.[47]

Mindful of these caveats, we may suggest the outlines of a picture of Solomon's royal cities.

At all three sites, especially Hazor and Megiddo, the Solomonic period was one of extensive building for fortification and government. At Hazor, a new casemate wall marked off one end of the earlier city, making a small but well-fortified garrison. Megiddo's walls apparently encompassed the entire mound, although this is not certain. At Gezer an earlier wall, originally built in the Late Bronze Age, was reinforced with a number of towers; and a section of casemate wall and a new gate were built, apparently in a gap where the older wall had been demolished.

Megiddo, with its several buildings, gives us our most complete picture of one of the new royal cities. The two elaborate palaces were certainly designed for a governor or for other high officials (Fig. 11). Traces of a similar palace or citadel were found at the western end of Hazor, and large structures uncovered by Macalister just to the west of the gate at Gezer need reexcavation to see if they also are Solomonic.[48] David Ussishkin's careful study of the biblical description of Solomon's palace in Jerusalem and of the Megiddo palaces has shown striking similarities between them and the *bīt-ḥilāni*, a building type from this period found in northern Syria and southern Anatolia.[49] This evidence of foreign architectural influence fits with the biblical account that the Solomonic temple in Jerusalem was built with the help of Phoenician craftsmen and suggests that Solomon's "foreign experts" were deeply involved in his building projects outside of Jerusalem as well.

A comparison of the three city gates raises an intriguing possibility. In the 1958 article in which Yadin identified the Solomonic gate at Gezer, he published a table of the measurements of the Hazor and Megiddo gates to show how similar they were to Gezer.[50] When the Gezer gate was finally excavated, the discrepancies diminished even more.[51] Thus Yadin's claim that the three gates were produced from

47. For a clear statement of the views of current historians on this point, see J. Maxwell Miller, *The Old Testament and the Historian* (London: SPCK, 1976), pp. 18–19.

48. *The Excavation of Gezer*, III, Plate VI. David Ussishkin has spotted another possibly Solomonic building at Gezer on the north side: "King Solomon's Palace and Building 1723 in Megiddo," *IEJ* 16 (1966):186, n. 36.

49. David Ussishkin, "King Solomon's Palaces," *BA* 36 (1973):78–105. See also his earlier article cited in the preceding note.

50. *IEJ* 8 (1958):86.

51. W. G. Dever et al., "Further Excavations at Gezer, 1967–71," *BA* 34 (1971): 112–20.

the same architectural plans does not seem far-fetched. True, the gates vary in detail—only the Gezer gate had benches lining the three interior bays—but the similarities are too many and too important to be fortuitous. Also instructive is a comparison of the Solomonic gates with one from the following century found at Lachish. The Lachish gate, although four-entry in type, is much larger.[52] Can one conclude that Solomon's government included something like a royal "corps of engineers" which planned and built fortifications all over the country out of a centralized bureaucracy? Such a proposal does not seem out of place against the biblical record of his reign, which details all kinds of governmental, fiscal, and commercial activities (1 Kings 3–11).

SOLOMON'S JERUSALEM

In turning to our last example, Jerusalem, we must decide whether to be very brief or very involved. For in the case of Jerusalem, we have extensive written accounts of Solomon's temple, his palace, and many of the objects made for the temple. It is legitimate to ask archaeology to suggest contemporary parallels for the elements described in that narrative: What might the temple have looked like? the bronze sea? the cherubim that were placed in the Holy of Holies? To approach the archaeology of Solomon's Jerusalem in this comparative way, however, would require far more space than we have available here. Therefore, we shall adhere to the more narrow approach which we adopted at the beginning, namely a summary of the results of actual excavation at the site.

Once we have decided to limit ourselves to Solomon's Jerusalem as revealed in the excavations, however, we find ourselves at the other extreme, with almost nothing to say. After decades of intensive excavation in Jerusalem, it is still unfortunately true that nothing has been found which on either stratigraphic or typological grounds—potsherds excepted—can with certainty be attributed to the age of Solomon. One possible exception is a ruined fragment of a casemate wall which Kathleen Kenyon found running north from the pre-Davidic walls of Jerusalem.[53] Although the stratigraphic evidence was insufficient to establish a sure date, a wall projected along this line would make good sense as the eastern wall of an expansion of the city between the pre-Davidic city and the temple mount (Fig. 12). However, the argument is tenuous and many doubt even this possibility.

52. David Ussishkin, "Excavations at Tel Lachish—1973–1977: Preliminary Report," *Tel Aviv* 5 (1978): 58 and Fig. 15.
53. Kathleen M. Kenyon, *Digging Up Jerusalem* (London: Ernest Benn, 1974), pp. 114–15. But see the postscript at the end of this chapter.

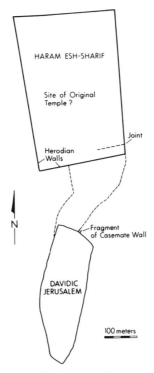

FIG. 12. SITES OF POSSIBLE
SOLOMONIC REMAINS IN
JERUSALEM

As for the Solomonic temple building itself or any of the governmental or even private structures of the Davidic–Solomonic period, not a trace remains. It is practically certain that the temple stood on the site now occupied by the Haram esh-Sharif with its structures, principally the Mosque of el-Aksa and the Dome of the Rock (Fig. 12). The outlines of the Haram, at least on the south and west, are composed of the great terrace walls which King Herod the Great built to support his new temple structures in the latter part of the last century B.C. The Jewish historian Josephus states that Herod doubled the size of the temple area, doubtless altering, perhaps burying, the foundations of the smaller temples of Solomon and Zerubbabel.[54] We might have

54. *The Jewish Wars* I.21.1, trans. H. St. J. Thackeray, *The Loeb Classical Library: Josephus,* vol. II (Cambridge, Mass.: Harvard University Press, 1961), p. 189. On the problem of the Herodian platform, see most recently David M. Jacobson, "The Plan of Herod's Temple," *PEQ* 112 (1980):33–40.

hoped for some trace of the Solomonic palace or other governmental structures to survive south of the present Haram; but all pre-Herodian occupation in the area was removed in antiquity, as revealed by both British and Israeli excavations. Therefore, unless excavations are some-day permitted within the bounds of the Haram itself, there is little hope of any archaeological recovery of the age of Solomon in Jerusalem.

One interesting recent theory should be mentioned, however. In the 1860s Charles Warren sank deep shafts from the surface and tunneled along the base of the east wall of the Haram, a method of investigation which, by the way, no responsible modern excavator would employ. Just north of the southeast corner he found a vertical joint in the masonry (Fig. 12). However, the upper courses of the wall have been rebuilt so many times over the centuries that nothing showed above ground; and his observation went unnoticed by most. In 1966, the Jordanian Department of Antiquities carried out a clearance along the east wall of the Haram and discovered that the seam runs all the way up from bedrock (Frontispiece B). To the left or south of the joint, the masonry consists of enormous blocks, carefully margined on all four sides of the exposed face and with a low smooth boss, the distinctive style of Herod's reconstruction. But to the right of the seam, the masonry is strikingly different. The stones are still large, 1.15 meters (4 ft.) high and up to 2 meters long (6 ft. 6 in.). But by no means do they approach the size of the Herodian blocks. Also the bosses of these smaller stones are different, with wider margins and higher and rougher centers. Finally, E.-M. Laperrousaz made careful measurements of the joint and found that it is not vertical but has a slight batter or slope from upper right to lower left of about 3 percent.[55] This means that the masonry to the left of the seam rests on and is supported by that on the right. Consequently, the rougher smaller masonry on the right cannot be a late repair but must be earlier than the time of Herod.

Thus far we have been describing what is observable, but as in so many archaeological problems the data permit more than one interpretation. Kenyon and Maurice Dunand were impressed by the similarity of the older masonry on the right of the seam to Persian-period structures in Lebanon and thus date it to the sixth century B.C.[56] If they are correct, this part of the wall would belong to the temple that was re-

---

55. E.-M. Laperrousaz, "A-t-on dégagé l'angle sud-est du «Temple de Salomon»?" *Syria* 50 (1973):360–65.
56. M. Dunand, "Byblos, Sidon, Jérusalem: Monuments apparentés des temps Aché-menides," *Supplements to Vetus Testamentum* 17 (1968):64–70; Kenyon, *Digging Up Jerusalem*, pp. 111–12.

built after the return from the Babylonian Exile (Ezra 6:14–15). Alternatively, Benjamin Mazar compares the earlier masonry typologically to stonework from the Hasmonean period, only a hundred years or so before Herod. Consequently, he attributes it to repairs effected at that time.[57] This issue will not be resolved without excavation, nor will the significance of the seam. But given the slight slope of the seam from north to south, it almost certainly marks the corner of the temple platform as Herod found it when he began his expansion. He then extended the podium to the south to its present size. If this reasoning is correct, then unless the returning exiles or later generations enlarged the Solomonic podium, which is not likely, the seam marks the site of the original corner of the Solomonic construction.

And so, ironically, the physical remains of Solomon's glory in Jerusalem reduce to two shadowy possibilities: a fragment of a casemate wall and a point marking the southeast corner of the temple platform—nothing more.

AUTHOR'S POSTSCRIPT

After the manuscript of this volume was submitted for publication late in the summer of 1980, there appeared press reports of the results of the 1980 season of excavations in Jerusalem which may greatly expand the picture of Solomonic Jerusalem described above. The director, Yigal Shiloh, announced discovery of massive structures which he dates to the period of David or Solomon. At this point, nothing more is known; and experienced scholars will be cautious until more evidence is available. No matter what the final verdict about Shiloh's new finds, the very possibility of such dramatic developments underscores the fact that synthesis of archaeological information is a ceaseless task, with today's "assured results" in jeopardy to tomorrow's new discovery.

57. Benjamin Mazar, *The Mountain of the Lord* (Garden City, N.Y.: Doubleday, 1975), p. 203.

V

The Future of
Biblical Archaeology

As we saw in Chapter I, biblical archaeology draws upon many disciplines besides Palestinian archaeology to carry out its task. The greatest of all biblical archaeologists, William F. Albright, once defined biblical archaeology as covering all the lands mentioned in the Bible, "from India to Spain, and from southern Russia to South Arabia and . . . the whole history of those lands from about 10,000 B.C., or even earlier, to the present time."[1] The sheer exuberance of such an all-encompassing definition strikes us as belonging to an earlier age of greater optimism and confidence in our ability to know all there is to know. In recent years the expansive biblical archaeology of Albright has given way to a more reflective mood for a number of reasons. We shall name here only three.

The first is the death within recent years of many of the greatest figures in the field of biblical archaeology: Yohanan Aharoni, Nelson Glueck, Kathleen Kenyon, Roland de Vaux, G. Ernest Wright, and of course Albright himself. No field can give up so many of its major figures within a brief span without suffering a sense of dislocation and loss of momentum. However temporary this period of adjustment, it is nevertheless painful.

A second reason for the mood of reappraisal within biblical archaeology is the tension created by the coming of age of Syro-Palestinian archaeology as a separate discipline independent of biblical studies. A similar parting of the ways took place between Mesopotamian studies and biblical studies earlier in this century. Much of the early interest in Mesopotamia was stimulated by the search for biblical parallels. But as the mass of data accumulated, particularly the collections of written tablets, fewer and fewer Assyriologists were willing to

1. William F. Albright, *Archaeology, Historical Analogy, and Early Biblical Tradition* (Baton Rouge: Louisiana State University Press, 1966), p. 13.

interrupt their own fascinating work to answer questions from biblical scholars. Something similar is now taking place in Palestinian archaeology. For increasing numbers of scholars, the motivating factors are purely historical or anthropological rather than biblical. Such a development is inevitable for many reasons; and if it will increase the range and depth of knowledge about ancient Palestine, it will be welcomed by all.

Along with the movement of Palestinian archaeology away from biblical studies, however, has come the suggestion of some that the term "biblical archaeology" be abandoned entirely and be replaced by "Syro-Palestinian archaeology." This suggestion must be stoutly rejected for an obvious reason: the focus of biblical archaeology is the Bible, not Palestine. To cite one other definition offered by Albright, biblical archaeology is "the systematic analysis or synthesis of any phase of biblical scholarship which can be clarified by archaeological discovery."[2] Many questions of an archaeological nature that one may wish to put to the Bible cannot be answered by Syro-Palestinian archaeology. One would have to turn to Mesopotamian archaeology, for example, to look for traces of exiled Israelites or Judeans. Biblical archaeology, like biblical form criticism or biblical anthropology, is a *biblical* discipline which exists for the benefit and interest of biblical studies. So long as people read the Bible and ask questions about the history and culture of the ancient world which produced it, those questions will have to be answered; and the sum total of those answers will comprise biblical archaeology. So although biblical archaeology anticipates a continuing close working relationship with its increasingly independent offspring, Palestinian archaeology, it must keep for itself the right to define itself and to set its own agenda.

The first two of the factors that are giving pause to biblical archaeology are temporary and will eventually pass. The third, however, is more serious and will get worse with time, not better. The fields from which biblical archaeology draws—Palestinian archaeology and epigraphy, Assyriology, and ancient Near Eastern studies in general—have experienced an information explosion, similar to the ones in so many other areas of human inquiry. The new tablets from Ebla are only the latest example of an unceasing flood of materials, much of it still unpublished, much more not yet adequately studied. In the field of Palestinian archaeology alone, the number of volumes published each year more than tripled in a recent ten-year period. There are

2. William F. Albright, "The Impact of Archaeology on Biblical Research—1966," *New Directions in Biblical Archaeology*, ed. D. N. Freedman and J. C. Greenfield (Garden City, N.Y.: Doubleday Anchor Books, 1971), pp. 3–4.

whole new models of synthesis of archaeological remains which stress sociological and anthropological approaches rather than the historical concerns that have dominated Near Eastern archaeology heretofore. These new models will force archaeologists to rethink methods and priorities and the way archaeological data are interpreted. We noted in Chapter III the lack of enough technical synthetic works in biblical archaeology, works that would pull together for the use of the biblical scholar results which are scattered through the journals. In short, we are being inundated by new data and new ideas and unmet needs.

How does one cope in such a flood? Is it any longer possible for a single individual to be a biblical archaeologist in the wider sense of Albright's first definition? Recent attempts to write comprehensive volumes in biblical archaeology have been criticized for the kind of lapse that occurs when a single author is trying to encompass more than he or she can competently control. The temptation, therefore, is to retreat into specialization, the sort of unhealthy narrowness that afflicts so many fields of inquiry. Surely this must be resisted. New models of team or collective investigation must be designed, parallel to the cooperative ventures that have long been customary in textual and translation projects.

With all its current problems, biblical archaeology remains one of the most exhilarating areas of study imaginable. Who can really complain about a field whose main problem is being swamped with new data and ideas? Archaeology helps to keep vital biblical scholarship as a whole. When all is said and done, few tasks in the study of the Bible can match it in excitement and importance, for it is the source of ever-new data to increase our ability to read the Bible with understanding and appreciation.

Appendix: The Archaeological Periods of Palestine

Printed below for reference and comparison are two influential systems of nomenclature for the archaeological periods of Palestine. The first is that of G. Ernest Wright from his article, "The Archaeology of Palestine" in *The Bible and the Ancient Near East*, ed. G. Ernest Wright (Garden City, N.Y.: Doubleday, 1961), pp. 73–112. In this article Wright does not deal with the periods before the Mesolithic or after 587 B.C. The second is the system adopted for Vol. IV of the *Encyclopedia of Archaeological Excavations in the Holy Land* (see *EAEHL* in list of abbreviations), p. 1226. Systems such as these are constantly being critiqued and refined in the light of new evidence and further reflection. There is an emerging consensus, for example, to begin the Iron II period at 1000 B.C. rather than at 900 B.C. with Wright.

Wright	*EAEHL*
	Paleolithic (Old Stone Age) 700,000–15,000 B.C.
Natufian (Mesolithic) ca. 10,000–8000 B.C.	Epipaleolithic (Middle Stone Age) 15,000–8300
Tahunian and Jerichoan (Neolithic) ca. 8000–5000 B.C.	Neolithic (New Stone Age) 8300–4500
Transition: Neolithic–Chalcolithic ca. 5000–4300 B.C.	Chalcolithic 4500–3100
Early Chalcolithic ca. 4300–3600 B.C.	
Ghassulian ca. 3600–3300 B.C.	

Early Bronze IA-C ca. 33rd–29th centuries B.C.	Early Bronze IA-C	3150–2850
Early Bronze II ca. 29th–27th centuries B.C.	Early Bronze II	2850–2650
Early Bronze III ca. 26th–24th centuries B.C.	Early Bronze III	2650–2350
Early Bronze IIIB ca. 24th–22nd centuries B.C.	Early Bronze IV (IIIA)	2350–2200
Middle Bronze I ca. 21st–20th centuries B.C.	Middle Bronze I	2200–2000
Middle Bronze IIA ca. 1900–1750/1700 B.C.	Middle Bronze IIA	2000–1750
Middle Bronze IIB ca. 1750/1700–1650/1625 B.C.	Middle Bronze IIB	1750–1550
Middle Bronze IIC ca. 1650/1625–1550/1500 B.C.		
Late Bronze I ca. 1500–1400 B.C.	Late Bronze I	1550–1400
Late Bronze IIA ca. 1400–1300 B.C.	Late Bronze IIA	1400–1300
Late Bronze IIB ca. 1300–1200 B.C.	Late Bronze IIB	1300–1200
Iron IA ca. 1200–1150 B.C.	Iron IA	1200–1150
Iron IB ca. 1150–1000 B.C.	Iron IB	1150–1000
Iron IC ca. 1000–900 B.C.		
Iron IIA ca. 900–800 B.C.	Iron IIA	1000–900
Iron IIB ca. 800–587 B.C.	Iron IIB	900–800
	Iron IIC	800–586
	Babylonian and Persian Periods 586–332	
	Hellenistic I	332–152
	Hellenistic II (Hasmonaean) 152–37	
	Roman I (Herodian) 37 B.C.–A.D. 70	
	Roman II	A.D. 70–180
	Roman III	180–324
	Byzantine I	324–451
	Byzantine II	451–640
	Early Arab	640–1099
	Crusader	1099–1291